C-952   CAREER EXAMINATION SERIES

This is your
PASSBOOK for...

Computer Technician

Test Preparation Study Guide
Questions & Answers

NATIONAL LEARNING CORPORATION®

COPYRIGHT NOTICE

This book is SOLELY intended for, is sold ONLY to, and its use is RESTRICTED to individual, bona fide applicants or candidates who qualify by virtue of having seriously filed applications for appropriate license, certificate, professional and/or promotional advancement, higher school matriculation, scholarship, or other legitimate requirements of education and/or governmental authorities.

This book is NOT intended for use, class instruction, tutoring, training, duplication, copying, reprinting, excerption, or adaptation, etc., by:

1) Other publishers
2) Proprietors and/or Instructors of "Coaching" and/or Preparatory Courses
3) Personnel and/or Training Divisions of commercial, industrial, and governmental organizations
4) Schools, colleges, or universities and/or their departments and staffs, including teachers and other personnel
5) Testing Agencies or Bureaus
6) Study groups which seek by the purchase of a single volume to copy and/or duplicate and/or adapt this material for use by the group as a whole without having purchased individual volumes for each of the members of the group
7) Et al.

Such persons would be in violation of appropriate Federal and State statutes.

PROVISION OF LICENSING AGREEMENTS – Recognized educational, commercial, industrial, and governmental institutions and organizations, and others legitimately engaged in educational pursuits, including training, testing, and measurement activities, may address request for a licensing agreement to the copyright owners, who will determine whether, and under what conditions, including fees and charges, the materials in this book may be used them. In other words, a licensing facility exists for the legitimate use of the material in this book on other than an individual basis. However, it is asseverated and affirmed here that the material in this book CANNOT be used without the receipt of the express permission of such a licensing agreement from the Publishers. Inquiries re licensing should be addressed to the company, attention rights and permissions department.

All rights reserved, including the right of reproduction in whole or in part, in any form or by any means, electronic or mechanical, including photocopying, recording, or by any information storage and retrieval system, without permission in writing from the Publisher.

Copyright © 2025 by
National Learning Corporation

212 Michael Drive, Syosset, NY 11791
(516) 921-8888 • www.passbooks.com
E-mail: info@passbooks.com

PASSBOOK® SERIES

THE *PASSBOOK® SERIES* has been created to prepare applicants and candidates for the ultimate academic battlefield – the examination room.

At some time in our lives, each and every one of us may be required to take an examination – for validation, matriculation, admission, qualification, registration, certification, or licensure.

Based on the assumption that every applicant or candidate has met the basic formal educational standards, has taken the required number of courses, and read the necessary texts, the *PASSBOOK® SERIES* furnishes the one special preparation which may assure passing with confidence, instead of failing with insecurity. Examination questions – together with answers – are furnished as the basic vehicle for study so that the mysteries of the examination and its compounding difficulties may be eliminated or diminished by a sure method.

This book is meant to help you pass your examination provided that you qualify and are serious in your objective.

The entire field is reviewed through the huge store of content information which is succinctly presented through a provocative and challenging approach – the question-and-answer method.

A climate of success is established by furnishing the correct answers at the end of each test.

You soon learn to recognize types of questions, forms of questions, and patterns of questioning. You may even begin to anticipate expected outcomes.

You perceive that many questions are repeated or adapted so that you can gain acute insights, which may enable you to score many sure points.

You learn how to confront new questions, or types of questions, and to attack them confidently and work out the correct answers.

You note objectives and emphases, and recognize pitfalls and dangers, so that you may make positive educational adjustments.

Moreover, you are kept fully informed in relation to new concepts, methods, practices, and directions in the field.

You discover that you are actually taking the examination all the time: you are preparing for the examination by "taking" an examination, not by reading extraneous and/or supererogatory textbooks.

In short, this PASSBOOK®, used directedly, should be an important factor in helping you to pass your test.

COMPUTER TECHNICIAN

DUTIES

Assists subscribers to a small computer system in using the system. Monitors computer and access equipment to isolate possible mechanical causes of difficulties encountered by system users. Provides elementary operating instructions to users not familiar with the system. Reviews user input and output to assist in correct terminal operation and to prevent improper or unscheduled use of the system. Runs diagnostic programs to ensure that the system is functioning correctly. Maintains a library of computer programs and resource material. Performs related work as required.

SCOPE OF THE EXAMINATION

The written test will cover knowledge, skills, and/or abilities in such areas as:
1. Understanding and interpreting written material, including technical computer information;
2. Basic personal computer hardware and software knowledge, including computer terminology;
3. Organizing data into tables and charts;
4. Office record keeping; and
5. Interpersonal relations.

HOW TO TAKE A TEST

I. YOU MUST PASS AN EXAMINATION

A. WHAT EVERY CANDIDATE SHOULD KNOW

Examination applicants often ask us for help in preparing for the written test. What can I study in advance? What kinds of questions will be asked? How will the test be given? How will the papers be graded?

As an applicant for a civil service examination, you may be wondering about some of these things. Our purpose here is to suggest effective methods of advance study and to describe civil service examinations.

Your chances for success on this examination can be increased if you know how to prepare. Those "pre-examination jitters" can be reduced if you know what to expect. You can even experience an adventure in good citizenship if you know why civil service exams are given.

B. WHY ARE CIVIL SERVICE EXAMINATIONS GIVEN?

Civil service examinations are important to you in two ways. As a citizen, you want public jobs filled by employees who know how to do their work. As a job seeker, you want a fair chance to compete for that job on an equal footing with other candidates. The best-known means of accomplishing this two-fold goal is the competitive examination.

Exams are widely publicized throughout the nation. They may be administered for jobs in federal, state, city, municipal, town or village governments or agencies.

Any citizen may apply, with some limitations, such as the age or residence of applicants. Your experience and education may be reviewed to see whether you meet the requirements for the particular examination. When these requirements exist, they are reasonable and applied consistently to all applicants. Thus, a competitive examination may cause you some uneasiness now, but it is your privilege and safeguard.

C. HOW ARE CIVIL SERVICE EXAMS DEVELOPED?

Examinations are carefully written by trained technicians who are specialists in the field known as "psychological measurement," in consultation with recognized authorities in the field of work that the test will cover. These experts recommend the subject matter areas or skills to be tested; only those knowledges or skills important to your success on the job are included. The most reliable books and source materials available are used as references. Together, the experts and technicians judge the difficulty level of the questions.

Test technicians know how to phrase questions so that the problem is clearly stated. Their ethics do not permit "trick" or "catch" questions. Questions may have been tried out on sample groups, or subjected to statistical analysis, to determine their usefulness.

Written tests are often used in combination with performance tests, ratings of training and experience, and oral interviews. All of these measures combine to form the best-known means of finding the right person for the right job.

II. HOW TO PASS THE WRITTEN TEST

A. NATURE OF THE EXAMINATION

To prepare intelligently for civil service examinations, you should know how they differ from school examinations you have taken. In school you were assigned certain definite pages to read or subjects to cover. The examination questions were quite detailed and usually emphasized memory. Civil service exams, on the other hand, try to discover your present ability to perform the duties of a position, plus your potentiality to learn these duties. In other words, a civil service exam attempts to predict how successful you will be. Questions cover such a broad area that they cannot be as minute and detailed as school exam questions.

In the public service similar kinds of work, or positions, are grouped together in one "class." This process is known as *position-classification*. All the positions in a class are paid according to the salary range for that class. One class title covers all of these positions, and they are all tested by the same examination.

B. FOUR BASIC STEPS

1) Study the announcement

How, then, can you know what subjects to study? Our best answer is: "Learn as much as possible about the class of positions for which you've applied." The exam will test the knowledge, skills and abilities needed to do the work.

Your most valuable source of information about the position you want is the official exam announcement. This announcement lists the training and experience qualifications. Check these standards and apply only if you come reasonably close to meeting them.

The brief description of the position in the examination announcement offers some clues to the subjects which will be tested. Think about the job itself. Review the duties in your mind. Can you perform them, or are there some in which you are rusty? Fill in the blank spots in your preparation.

Many jurisdictions preview the written test in the exam announcement by including a section called "Knowledge and Abilities Required," "Scope of the Examination," or some similar heading. Here you will find out specifically what fields will be tested.

2) Review your own background

Once you learn in general what the position is all about, and what you need to know to do the work, ask yourself which subjects you already know fairly well and which need improvement. You may wonder whether to concentrate on improving your strong areas or on building some background in your fields of weakness. When the announcement has specified "some knowledge" or "considerable knowledge," or has used adjectives like "beginning principles of..." or "advanced ... methods," you can get a clue as to the number and difficulty of questions to be asked in any given field. More questions, and hence broader coverage, would be included for those subjects which are more important in the work. Now weigh your strengths and weaknesses against the job requirements and prepare accordingly.

3) Determine the level of the position

Another way to tell how intensively you should prepare is to understand the level of the job for which you are applying. Is it the entering level? In other words, is this the position in which beginners in a field of work are hired? Or is it an intermediate or advanced level? Sometimes this is indicated by such words as "Junior" or "Senior" in the class title. Other jurisdictions use Roman numerals to designate the level – Clerk I, Clerk II, for example. The word "Supervisor" sometimes appears in the title. If the level is not indicated by the title, check the description of duties. Will you be working under very close supervision, or will you have responsibility for independent decisions in this work?

4) Choose appropriate study materials

Now that you know the subjects to be examined and the relative amount of each subject to be covered, you can choose suitable study materials. For beginning level jobs, or even advanced ones, if you have a pronounced weakness in some aspect of your training, read a modern, standard textbook in that field. Be sure it is up to date and has general coverage. Such books are normally available at your library, and the librarian will be glad to help you locate one. For entry-level positions, questions of appropriate difficulty are chosen – neither highly advanced questions, nor those too simple. Such questions require careful thought but not advanced training.

If the position for which you are applying is technical or advanced, you will read more advanced, specialized material. If you are already familiar with the basic principles of your field, elementary textbooks would waste your time. Concentrate on advanced textbooks and technical periodicals. Think through the concepts and review difficult problems in your field.

These are all general sources. You can get more ideas on your own initiative, following these leads. For example, training manuals and publications of the government agency which employs workers in your field can be useful, particularly for technical and professional positions. A letter or visit to the government department involved may result in more specific study suggestions, and certainly will provide you with a more definite idea of the exact nature of the position you are seeking.

III. KINDS OF TESTS

Tests are used for purposes other than measuring knowledge and ability to perform specified duties. For some positions, it is equally important to test ability to make adjustments to new situations or to profit from training. In others, basic mental abilities not dependent on information are essential. Questions which test these things may not appear as pertinent to the duties of the position as those which test for knowledge and information. Yet they are often highly important parts of a fair examination. For very general questions, it is almost impossible to help you direct your study efforts. What we can do is to point out some of the more common of these general abilities needed in public service positions and describe some typical questions.

1) General information

Broad, general information has been found useful for predicting job success in some kinds of work. This is tested in a variety of ways, from vocabulary lists to questions about current events. Basic background in some field of work, such as sociology or economics, may be sampled in a group of questions. Often these are principles which have become familiar to most persons through exposure rather than through formal training. It is difficult to advise you how to study for these questions; being alert to the world around you is our best suggestion.

2) Verbal ability

An example of an ability needed in many positions is verbal or language ability. Verbal ability is, in brief, the ability to use and understand words. Vocabulary and grammar tests are typical measures of this ability. Reading comprehension or paragraph interpretation questions are common in many kinds of civil service tests. You are given a paragraph of written material and asked to find its central meaning.

3) Numerical ability
Number skills can be tested by the familiar arithmetic problem, by checking paired lists of numbers to see which are alike and which are different, or by interpreting charts and graphs. In the latter test, a graph may be printed in the test booklet which you are asked to use as the basis for answering questions.

4) Observation
A popular test for law-enforcement positions is the observation test. A picture is shown to you for several minutes, then taken away. Questions about the picture test your ability to observe both details and larger elements.

5) Following directions
In many positions in the public service, the employee must be able to carry out written instructions dependably and accurately. You may be given a chart with several columns, each column listing a variety of information. The questions require you to carry out directions involving the information given in the chart.

6) Skills and aptitudes
Performance tests effectively measure some manual skills and aptitudes. When the skill is one in which you are trained, such as typing or shorthand, you can practice. These tests are often very much like those given in business school or high school courses. For many of the other skills and aptitudes, however, no short-time preparation can be made. Skills and abilities natural to you or that you have developed throughout your lifetime are being tested.

Many of the general questions just described provide all the data needed to answer the questions and ask you to use your reasoning ability to find the answers. Your best preparation for these tests, as well as for tests of facts and ideas, is to be at your physical and mental best. You, no doubt, have your own methods of getting into an exam-taking mood and keeping "in shape." The next section lists some ideas on this subject.

IV. KINDS OF QUESTIONS

Only rarely is the "essay" question, which you answer in narrative form, used in civil service tests. Civil service tests are usually of the short-answer type. Full instructions for answering these questions will be given to you at the examination. But in case this is your first experience with short-answer questions and separate answer sheets, here is what you need to know:

1) Multiple-choice Questions
Most popular of the short-answer questions is the "multiple choice" or "best answer" question. It can be used, for example, to test for factual knowledge, ability to solve problems or judgment in meeting situations found at work.
A multiple-choice question is normally one of three types—
- It can begin with an incomplete statement followed by several possible endings. You are to find the one ending which *best* completes the statement, although some of the others may not be entirely wrong.
- It can also be a complete statement in the form of a question which is answered by choosing one of the statements listed.

- It can be in the form of a problem – again you select the best answer.

Here is an example of a multiple-choice question with a discussion which should give you some clues as to the method for choosing the right answer:

When an employee has a complaint about his assignment, the action which will *best* help him overcome his difficulty is to
- A. discuss his difficulty with his coworkers
- B. take the problem to the head of the organization
- C. take the problem to the person who gave him the assignment
- D. say nothing to anyone about his complaint

In answering this question, you should study each of the choices to find which is best. Consider choice "A" – Certainly an employee may discuss his complaint with fellow employees, but no change or improvement can result, and the complaint remains unresolved. Choice "B" is a poor choice since the head of the organization probably does not know what assignment you have been given, and taking your problem to him is known as "going over the head" of the supervisor. The supervisor, or person who made the assignment, is the person who can clarify it or correct any injustice. Choice "C" is, therefore, correct. To say nothing, as in choice "D," is unwise. Supervisors have and interest in knowing the problems employees are facing, and the employee is seeking a solution to his problem.

2) True/False Questions

The "true/false" or "right/wrong" form of question is sometimes used. Here a complete statement is given. Your job is to decide whether the statement is right or wrong.

SAMPLE: A roaming cell-phone call to a nearby city costs less than a non-roaming call to a distant city.

This statement is wrong, or false, since roaming calls are more expensive.

This is not a complete list of all possible question forms, although most of the others are variations of these common types. You will always get complete directions for answering questions. Be sure you understand *how* to mark your answers – ask questions until you do.

V. RECORDING YOUR ANSWERS

Computer terminals are used more and more today for many different kinds of exams.

For an examination with very few applicants, you may be told to record your answers in the test booklet itself. Separate answer sheets are much more common. If this separate answer sheet is to be scored by machine – and this is often the case – it is highly important that you mark your answers correctly in order to get credit.

An electronic scoring machine is often used in civil service offices because of the speed with which papers can be scored. Machine-scored answer sheets must be marked with a pencil, which will be given to you. This pencil has a high graphite content which responds to the electronic scoring machine. As a matter of fact, stray dots may register as answers, so do not let your pencil rest on the answer sheet while you are pondering the correct answer. Also, if your pencil lead breaks or is otherwise defective, ask for another.

Since the answer sheet will be dropped in a slot in the scoring machine, be careful not to bend the corners or get the paper crumpled.

The answer sheet normally has five vertical columns of numbers, with 30 numbers to a column. These numbers correspond to the question numbers in your test booklet. After each number, going across the page are four or five pairs of dotted lines. These short dotted lines have small letters or numbers above them. The first two pairs may also have a "T" or "F" above the letters. This indicates that the first two pairs only are to be used if the questions are of the true-false type. If the questions are multiple choice, disregard the "T" and "F" and pay attention only to the small letters or numbers.

Answer your questions in the manner of the sample that follows:

32. The largest city in the United States is
    A. Washington, D.C.
    B. New York City
    C. Chicago
    D. Detroit
    E. San Francisco

1) Choose the answer you think is best. (New York City is the largest, so "B" is correct.)
2) Find the row of dotted lines numbered the same as the question you are answering. (Find row number 32)
3) Find the pair of dotted lines corresponding to the answer. (Find the pair of lines under the mark "B.")
4) Make a solid black mark between the dotted lines.

VI. BEFORE THE TEST

Common sense will help you find procedures to follow to get ready for an examination. Too many of us, however, overlook these sensible measures. Indeed, nervousness and fatigue have been found to be the most serious reasons why applicants fail to do their best on civil service tests. Here is a list of reminders:

- Begin your preparation early – Don't wait until the last minute to go scurrying around for books and materials or to find out what the position is all about.
- Prepare continuously – An hour a night for a week is better than an all-night cram session. This has been definitely established. What is more, a night a week for a month will return better dividends than crowding your study into a shorter period of time.
- Locate the place of the exam – You have been sent a notice telling you when and where to report for the examination. If the location is in a different town or otherwise unfamiliar to you, it would be well to inquire the best route and learn something about the building.
- Relax the night before the test – Allow your mind to rest. Do not study at all that night. Plan some mild recreation or diversion; then go to bed early and get a good night's sleep.
- Get up early enough to make a leisurely trip to the place for the test – This way unforeseen events, traffic snarls, unfamiliar buildings, etc. will not upset you.
- Dress comfortably – A written test is not a fashion show. You will be known by number and not by name, so wear something comfortable.

- Leave excess paraphernalia at home – Shopping bags and odd bundles will get in your way. You need bring only the items mentioned in the official notice you received; usually everything you need is provided. Do not bring reference books to the exam. They will only confuse those last minutes and be taken away from you when in the test room.
- Arrive somewhat ahead of time – If because of transportation schedules you must get there very early, bring a newspaper or magazine to take your mind off yourself while waiting.
- Locate the examination room – When you have found the proper room, you will be directed to the seat or part of the room where you will sit. Sometimes you are given a sheet of instructions to read while you are waiting. Do not fill out any forms until you are told to do so; just read them and be prepared.
- Relax and prepare to listen to the instructions
- If you have any physical problem that may keep you from doing your best, be sure to tell the test administrator. If you are sick or in poor health, you really cannot do your best on the exam. You can come back and take the test some other time.

VII. AT THE TEST

The day of the test is here and you have the test booklet in your hand. The temptation to get going is very strong. Caution! There is more to success than knowing the right answers. You must know how to identify your papers and understand variations in the type of short-answer question used in this particular examination. Follow these suggestions for maximum results from your efforts:

1) Cooperate with the monitor

The test administrator has a duty to create a situation in which you can be as much at ease as possible. He will give instructions, tell you when to begin, check to see that you are marking your answer sheet correctly, and so on. He is not there to guard you, although he will see that your competitors do not take unfair advantage. He wants to help you do your best.

2) Listen to all instructions

Don't jump the gun! Wait until you understand all directions. In most civil service tests you get more time than you need to answer the questions. So don't be in a hurry. Read each word of instructions until you clearly understand the meaning. Study the examples, listen to all announcements and follow directions. Ask questions if you do not understand what to do.

3) Identify your papers

Civil service exams are usually identified by number only. You will be assigned a number; you must not put your name on your test papers. Be sure to copy your number correctly. Since more than one exam may be given, copy your exact examination title.

4) Plan your time

Unless you are told that a test is a "speed" or "rate of work" test, speed itself is usually not important. Time enough to answer all the questions will be provided, but this does not mean that you have all day. An overall time limit has been set. Divide the total time (in minutes) by the number of questions to determine the approximate time you have for each question.

5) Do not linger over difficult questions

If you come across a difficult question, mark it with a paper clip (useful to have along) and come back to it when you have been through the booklet. One caution if you do this – be sure to skip a number on your answer sheet as well. Check often to be sure that you have not lost your place and that you are marking in the row numbered the same as the question you are answering.

6) Read the questions

Be sure you know what the question asks! Many capable people are unsuccessful because they failed to *read* the questions correctly.

7) Answer all questions

Unless you have been instructed that a penalty will be deducted for incorrect answers, it is better to guess than to omit a question.

8) Speed tests

It is often better NOT to guess on speed tests. It has been found that on timed tests people are tempted to spend the last few seconds before time is called in marking answers at random – without even reading them – in the hope of picking up a few extra points. To discourage this practice, the instructions may warn you that your score will be "corrected" for guessing. That is, a penalty will be applied. The incorrect answers will be deducted from the correct ones, or some other penalty formula will be used.

9) Review your answers

If you finish before time is called, go back to the questions you guessed or omitted to give them further thought. Review other answers if you have time.

10) Return your test materials

If you are ready to leave before others have finished or time is called, take ALL your materials to the monitor and leave quietly. Never take any test material with you. The monitor can discover whose papers are not complete, and taking a test booklet may be grounds for disqualification.

VIII. EXAMINATION TECHNIQUES

1) Read the general instructions carefully. These are usually printed on the first page of the exam booklet. As a rule, these instructions refer to the timing of the examination; the fact that you should not start work until the signal and must stop work at a signal, etc. If there are any *special* instructions, such as a choice of questions to be answered, make sure that you note this instruction carefully.

2) When you are ready to start work on the examination, that is as soon as the signal has been given, read the instructions to each question booklet, underline any key words or phrases, such as *least, best, outline, describe* and the like. In this way you will tend to answer as requested rather than discover on reviewing your paper that you *listed without describing*, that you selected the *worst* choice rather than the *best* choice, etc.

3) If the examination is of the objective or multiple-choice type – that is, each question will also give a series of possible answers: A, B, C or D, and you are called upon to select the best answer and write the letter next to that answer on your answer paper – it is advisable to start answering each question in turn. There may be anywhere from 50 to 100 such questions in the three or four hours allotted and you can see how much time would be taken if you read through all the questions before beginning to answer any. Furthermore, if you come across a question or group of questions which you know would be difficult to answer, it would undoubtedly affect your handling of all the other questions.

4) If the examination is of the essay type and contains but a few questions, it is a moot point as to whether you should read all the questions before starting to answer any one. Of course, if you are given a choice – say five out of seven and the like – then it is essential to read all the questions so you can eliminate the two that are most difficult. If, however, you are asked to answer all the questions, there may be danger in trying to answer the easiest one first because you may find that you will spend too much time on it. The best technique is to answer the first question, then proceed to the second, etc.

5) Time your answers. Before the exam begins, write down the time it started, then add the time allowed for the examination and write down the time it must be completed, then divide the time available somewhat as follows:
    - If 3-1/2 hours are allowed, that would be 210 minutes. If you have 80 objective-type questions, that would be an average of 2-1/2 minutes per question. Allow yourself no more than 2 minutes per question, or a total of 160 minutes, which will permit about 50 minutes to review.
    - If for the time allotment of 210 minutes there are 7 essay questions to answer, that would average about 30 minutes a question. Give yourself only 25 minutes per question so that you have about 35 minutes to review.

6) The most important instruction is to *read each question* and make sure you know what is wanted. The second most important instruction is to *time yourself properly* so that you answer every question. The third most important instruction is to *answer every question*. Guess if you have to but include something for each question. Remember that you will receive no credit for a blank and will probably receive some credit if you write something in answer to an essay question. If you guess a letter – say "B" for a multiple-choice question – you may have guessed right. If you leave a blank as an answer to a multiple-choice question, the examiners may respect your feelings but it will not add a point to your score. Some exams may penalize you for wrong answers, so in such cases *only*, you may not want to guess unless you have some basis for your answer.

7) Suggestions
    a. Objective-type questions
       1. Examine the question booklet for proper sequence of pages and questions
       2. Read all instructions carefully
       3. Skip any question which seems too difficult; return to it after all other questions have been answered
       4. Apportion your time properly; do not spend too much time on any single question or group of questions

5. Note and underline key words – *all, most, fewest, least, best, worst, same, opposite,* etc.
6. Pay particular attention to negatives
7. Note unusual option, e.g., unduly long, short, complex, different or similar in content to the body of the question
8. Observe the use of "hedging" words – *probably, may, most likely,* etc.
9. Make sure that your answer is put next to the same number as the question
10. Do not second-guess unless you have good reason to believe the second answer is definitely more correct
11. Cross out original answer if you decide another answer is more accurate; do not erase until you are ready to hand your paper in
12. Answer all questions; guess unless instructed otherwise
13. Leave time for review

  b. Essay questions
1. Read each question carefully
2. Determine exactly what is wanted. Underline key words or phrases.
3. Decide on outline or paragraph answer
4. Include many different points and elements unless asked to develop any one or two points or elements
5. Show impartiality by giving pros and cons unless directed to select one side only
6. Make and write down any assumptions you find necessary to answer the questions
7. Watch your English, grammar, punctuation and choice of words
8. Time your answers; don't crowd material

8) Answering the essay question

Most essay questions can be answered by framing the specific response around several key words or ideas. Here are a few such key words or ideas:

M's: manpower, materials, methods, money, management
P's: purpose, program, policy, plan, procedure, practice, problems, pitfalls, personnel, public relations

  a. Six basic steps in handling problems:
1. Preliminary plan and background development
2. Collect information, data and facts
3. Analyze and interpret information, data and facts
4. Analyze and develop solutions as well as make recommendations
5. Prepare report and sell recommendations
6. Install recommendations and follow up effectiveness

  b. Pitfalls to avoid
1. *Taking things for granted* – A statement of the situation does not necessarily imply that each of the elements is necessarily true; for example, a complaint may be invalid and biased so that all that can be taken for granted is that a complaint has been registered

2. *Considering only one side of a situation* – Wherever possible, indicate several alternatives and then point out the reasons you selected the best one
3. *Failing to indicate follow up* – Whenever your answer indicates action on your part, make certain that you will take proper follow-up action to see how successful your recommendations, procedures or actions turn out to be
4. *Taking too long in answering any single question* – Remember to time your answers properly

IX. AFTER THE TEST

Scoring procedures differ in detail among civil service jurisdictions although the general principles are the same. Whether the papers are hand-scored or graded by machine we have described, they are nearly always graded by number. That is, the person who marks the paper knows only the number – never the name – of the applicant. Not until all the papers have been graded will they be matched with names. If other tests, such as training and experience or oral interview ratings have been given, scores will be combined. Different parts of the examination usually have different weights. For example, the written test might count 60 percent of the final grade, and a rating of training and experience 40 percent. In many jurisdictions, veterans will have a certain number of points added to their grades.

After the final grade has been determined, the names are placed in grade order and an eligible list is established. There are various methods for resolving ties between those who get the same final grade – probably the most common is to place first the name of the person whose application was received first. Job offers are made from the eligible list in the order the names appear on it. You will be notified of your grade and your rank as soon as all these computations have been made. This will be done as rapidly as possible.

People who are found to meet the requirements in the announcement are called "eligibles." Their names are put on a list of eligible candidates. An eligible's chances of getting a job depend on how high he stands on this list and how fast agencies are filling jobs from the list.

When a job is to be filled from a list of eligibles, the agency asks for the names of people on the list of eligibles for that job. When the civil service commission receives this request, it sends to the agency the names of the three people highest on this list. Or, if the job to be filled has specialized requirements, the office sends the agency the names of the top three persons who meet these requirements from the general list.

The appointing officer makes a choice from among the three people whose names were sent to him. If the selected person accepts the appointment, the names of the others are put back on the list to be considered for future openings.

That is the rule in hiring from all kinds of eligible lists, whether they are for typist, carpenter, chemist, or something else. For every vacancy, the appointing officer has his choice of any one of the top three eligibles on the list. This explains why the person whose name is on top of the list sometimes does not get an appointment when some of the persons lower on the list do. If the appointing officer chooses the second or third eligible, the No. 1 eligible does not get a job at once, but stays on the list until he is appointed or the list is terminated.

X. HOW TO PASS THE INTERVIEW TEST

The examination for which you applied requires an oral interview test. You have already taken the written test and you are now being called for the interview test – the final part of the formal examination.

You may think that it is not possible to prepare for an interview test and that there are no procedures to follow during an interview. Our purpose is to point out some things you can do in advance that will help you and some good rules to follow and pitfalls to avoid while you are being interviewed.

What is an interview supposed to test?

The written examination is designed to test the technical knowledge and competence of the candidate; the oral is designed to evaluate intangible qualities, not readily measured otherwise, and to establish a list showing the relative fitness of each candidate – as measured against his competitors – for the position sought. Scoring is not on the basis of "right" and "wrong," but on a sliding scale of values ranging from "not passable" to "outstanding." As a matter of fact, it is possible to achieve a relatively low score without a single "incorrect" answer because of evident weakness in the qualities being measured.

Occasionally, an examination may consist entirely of an oral test – either an individual or a group oral. In such cases, information is sought concerning the technical knowledges and abilities of the candidate, since there has been no written examination for this purpose. More commonly, however, an oral test is used to supplement a written examination.

Who conducts interviews?

The composition of oral boards varies among different jurisdictions. In nearly all, a representative of the personnel department serves as chairman. One of the members of the board may be a representative of the department in which the candidate would work. In some cases, "outside experts" are used, and, frequently, a businessman or some other representative of the general public is asked to serve. Labor and management or other special groups may be represented. The aim is to secure the services of experts in the appropriate field.

However the board is composed, it is a good idea (and not at all improper or unethical) to ascertain in advance of the interview who the members are and what groups they represent. When you are introduced to them, you will have some idea of their backgrounds and interests, and at least you will not stutter and stammer over their names.

What should be done before the interview?

While knowledge about the board members is useful and takes some of the surprise element out of the interview, there is other preparation which is more substantive. It *is* possible to prepare for an oral interview – in several ways:

1) Keep a copy of your application and review it carefully before the interview

This may be the only document before the oral board, and the starting point of the interview. Know what education and experience you have listed there, and the sequence and dates of all of it. Sometimes the board will ask you to review the highlights of your experience for them; you should not have to hem and haw doing it.

2) Study the class specification and the examination announcement

Usually, the oral board has one or both of these to guide them. The qualities, characteristics or knowledges required by the position sought are stated in these documents. They offer valuable clues as to the nature of the oral interview. For example, if the job involves supervisory responsibilities, the announcement will usually indicate that knowledge of modern supervisory methods and the qualifications of the candidate as a supervisor will be tested. If so, you can expect such questions, frequently in the form of a hypothetical situation which you are expected to solve. NEVER go into an oral without knowledge of the duties and responsibilities of the job you seek.

3) Think through each qualification required

Try to visualize the kind of questions you would ask if you were a board member. How well could you answer them? Try especially to appraise your own knowledge and background in each area, *measured against the job sought*, and identify any areas in which you are weak. Be critical and realistic – do not flatter yourself.

4) Do some general reading in areas in which you feel you may be weak

For example, if the job involves supervision and your past experience has NOT, some general reading in supervisory methods and practices, particularly in the field of human relations, might be useful. Do NOT study agency procedures or detailed manuals. The oral board will be testing your understanding and capacity, not your memory.

5) Get a good night's sleep and watch your general health and mental attitude

You will want a clear head at the interview. Take care of a cold or any other minor ailment, and of course, no hangovers.

What should be done on the day of the interview?

Now comes the day of the interview itself. Give yourself plenty of time to get there. Plan to arrive somewhat ahead of the scheduled time, particularly if your appointment is in the fore part of the day. If a previous candidate fails to appear, the board might be ready for you a bit early. By early afternoon an oral board is almost invariably behind schedule if there are many candidates, and you may have to wait. Take along a book or magazine to read, or your application to review, but leave any extraneous material in the waiting room when you go in for your interview. In any event, relax and compose yourself.

The matter of dress is important. The board is forming impressions about you – from your experience, your manners, your attitude, and your appearance. Give your personal appearance careful attention. Dress your best, but not your flashiest. Choose conservative, appropriate clothing, and be sure it is immaculate. This is a business interview, and your appearance should indicate that you regard it as such. Besides, being well groomed and properly dressed will help boost your confidence.

Sooner or later, someone will call your name and escort you into the interview room. *This is it.* From here on you are on your own. It is too late for any more preparation. But remember, you asked for this opportunity to prove your fitness, and you are here because your request was granted.

What happens when you go in?

The usual sequence of events will be as follows: The clerk (who is often the board stenographer) will introduce you to the chairman of the oral board, who will introduce you to the other members of the board. Acknowledge the introductions before you sit down. Do not be surprised if you find a microphone facing you or a stenotypist sitting by. Oral interviews are usually recorded in the event of an appeal or other review.

Usually the chairman of the board will open the interview by reviewing the highlights of your education and work experience from your application – primarily for the benefit of the other members of the board, as well as to get the material into the record. Do not interrupt or comment unless there is an error or significant misinterpretation; if that is the case, do not hesitate. But do not quibble about insignificant matters. Also, he will usually ask you some question about your education, experience or your present job – partly to get you to start talking and to establish the interviewing "rapport." He may start the actual questioning, or turn it over to one of the other members. Frequently, each member undertakes the questioning on a particular area, one in which he is perhaps most competent, so you can expect each member to participate in the examination. Because time is limited, you may also expect some rather abrupt switches in the direction the questioning takes, so do not be upset by it. Normally, a board member will not pursue a single line of questioning unless he discovers a particular strength or weakness.

After each member has participated, the chairman will usually ask whether any member has any further questions, then will ask you if you have anything you wish to add. Unless you are expecting this question, it may floor you. Worse, it may start you off on an extended, extemporaneous speech. The board is not usually seeking more information. The question is principally to offer you a last opportunity to present further qualifications or to indicate that you have nothing to add. So, if you feel that a significant qualification or characteristic has been overlooked, it is proper to point it out in a sentence or so. Do not compliment the board on the thoroughness of their examination – they have been sketchy, and you know it. If you wish, merely say, "No thank you, I have nothing further to add." This is a point where you can "talk yourself out" of a good impression or fail to present an important bit of information. Remember, *you close the interview yourself*.

The chairman will then say, "That is all, Mr. _____, thank you." Do not be startled; the interview is over, and quicker than you think. Thank him, gather your belongings and take your leave. Save your sigh of relief for the other side of the door.

How to put your best foot forward

Throughout this entire process, you may feel that the board individually and collectively is trying to pierce your defenses, seek out your hidden weaknesses and embarrass and confuse you. Actually, this is not true. They are obliged to make an appraisal of your qualifications for the job you are seeking, and they want to see you in your best light. Remember, they must interview all candidates and a non-cooperative candidate may become a failure in spite of their best efforts to bring out his qualifications. Here are 15 suggestions that will help you:

1) Be natural – Keep your attitude confident, not cocky

If you are not confident that you can do the job, do not expect the board to be. Do not apologize for your weaknesses, try to bring out your strong points. The board is interested in a positive, not negative, presentation. Cockiness will antagonize any board member and make him wonder if you are covering up a weakness by a false show of strength.

2) Get comfortable, but don't lounge or sprawl

Sit erectly but not stiffly. A careless posture may lead the board to conclude that you are careless in other things, or at least that you are not impressed by the importance of the occasion. Either conclusion is natural, even if incorrect. Do not fuss with your clothing, a pencil or an ashtray. Your hands may occasionally be useful to emphasize a point; do not let them become a point of distraction.

3) Do not wisecrack or make small talk

This is a serious situation, and your attitude should show that you consider it as such. Further, the time of the board is limited – they do not want to waste it, and neither should you.

4) Do not exaggerate your experience or abilities
In the first place, from information in the application or other interviews and sources, the board may know more about you than you think. Secondly, you probably will not get away with it. An experienced board is rather adept at spotting such a situation, so do not take the chance.

5) If you know a board member, do not make a point of it, yet do not hide it
Certainly you are not fooling him, and probably not the other members of the board. Do not try to take advantage of your acquaintanceship – it will probably do you little good.

6) Do not dominate the interview
Let the board do that. They will give you the clues – do not assume that you have to do all the talking. Realize that the board has a number of questions to ask you, and do not try to take up all the interview time by showing off your extensive knowledge of the answer to the first one.

7) Be attentive
You only have 20 minutes or so, and you should keep your attention at its sharpest throughout. When a member is addressing a problem or question to you, give him your undivided attention. Address your reply principally to him, but do not exclude the other board members.

8) Do not interrupt
A board member may be stating a problem for you to analyze. He will ask you a question when the time comes. Let him state the problem, and wait for the question.

9) Make sure you understand the question
Do not try to answer until you are sure what the question is. If it is not clear, restate it in your own words or ask the board member to clarify it for you. However, do not haggle about minor elements.

10) Reply promptly but not hastily
A common entry on oral board rating sheets is "candidate responded readily," or "candidate hesitated in replies." Respond as promptly and quickly as you can, but do not jump to a hasty, ill-considered answer.

11) Do not be peremptory in your answers
A brief answer is proper – but do not fire your answer back. That is a losing game from your point of view. The board member can probably ask questions much faster than you can answer them.

12) Do not try to create the answer you think the board member wants
He is interested in what kind of mind you have and how it works – not in playing games. Furthermore, he can usually spot this practice and will actually grade you down on it.

13) Do not switch sides in your reply merely to agree with a board member
Frequently, a member will take a contrary position merely to draw you out and to see if you are willing and able to defend your point of view. Do not start a debate, yet do not surrender a good position. If a position is worth taking, it is worth defending.

14) Do not be afraid to admit an error in judgment if you are shown to be wrong

The board knows that you are forced to reply without any opportunity for careful consideration. Your answer may be demonstrably wrong. If so, admit it and get on with the interview.

15) Do not dwell at length on your present job

The opening question may relate to your present assignment. Answer the question but do not go into an extended discussion. You are being examined for a *new* job, not your present one. As a matter of fact, try to phrase ALL your answers in terms of the job for which you are being examined.

Basis of Rating

Probably you will forget most of these "do's" and "don'ts" when you walk into the oral interview room. Even remembering them all will not ensure you a passing grade. Perhaps you did not have the qualifications in the first place. But remembering them will help you to put your best foot forward, without treading on the toes of the board members.

Rumor and popular opinion to the contrary notwithstanding, an oral board wants you to make the best appearance possible. They know you are under pressure – but they also want to see how you respond to it as a guide to what your reaction would be under the pressures of the job you seek. They will be influenced by the degree of poise you display, the personal traits you show and the manner in which you respond.

ABOUT THIS BOOK

This book contains tests divided into Examination Sections. Go through each test, answering every question in the margin. We have also attached a sample answer sheet at the back of the book that can be removed and used. At the end of each test look at the answer key and check your answers. On the ones you got wrong, look at the right answer choice and learn. Do not fill in the answers first. Do not memorize the questions and answers, but understand the answer and principles involved. On your test, the questions will likely be different from the samples. Questions are changed and new ones added. If you understand these past questions you should have success with any changes that arise. Tests may consist of several types of questions. We have additional books on each subject should more study be advisable or necessary for you. Finally, the more you study, the better prepared you will be. This book is intended to be the last thing you study before you walk into the examination room. Prior study of relevant texts is also recommended. NLC publishes some of these in our Fundamental Series. Knowledge and good sense are important factors in passing your exam. Good luck also helps. So now study this Passbook, absorb the material contained within and take that knowledge into the examination. Then do your best to pass that exam.

EXAMINATION SECTION

EXAMINATION SECTION
TEST 1

DIRECTIONS: Each question or incomplete statement is followed by several suggested answers or completions. Select the one that BEST answers the question or completes the statement. *PRINT THE LETTER OF THE CORRECT ANSWER IN THE SPACE AT THE RIGHT.*

1. Which one of the following is considered a word processor program? 1.____
   - A. Microsoft Word
   - B. Microsoft Works
   - C. Notepad
   - D. Both A and B

2. Default headings are available under the _____ tab. 2.____
   - A. Insert
   - B. Home
   - C. File
   - D. View

3. _____ deals with font, alignment and margins. 3.____
   - A. Selecting
   - B. Formatting
   - C. Composing
   - D. Pattern

4. Which one of the following is the BEST format for storing bit-mapped images on the computer? 4.____
   - A. .JPG
   - B. .PNG
   - C. .GIF
   - D. .TIF

5. A header specifies an area in the _____ margins of every page. 5.____
   - A. top
   - B. bottom
   - C. left
   - D. right

6. When an Excel file is inserted into a Word document, the data is 6.____
   - A. hyperlinked
   - B. placed in a Word table
   - C. linked
   - D. embedded

7. A workbook in Excel is a file that 7.____
   - A. is primarily used to generate graphs
   - B. is often used for word processing
   - C. can contain many sheets, chart sheets and worksheets
   - D. both A and B

8. Excel can produce chart types that include 8.____
   - A. only line graphs
   - B. bar charts, line graphs and pie charts
   - C. line graphs and pie charts only
   - D. bar charts and line graphs only

9. In PowerPoint, the motion path is a 9.____
   - A. method of moving items on the slide
   - B. method of advancing slides
   - C. indentation
   - D. type of animation

10. _____ replaces similar words in a document.
    A. Word Count   B. Thesaurus   C. Wrap Text   D. Format Printer

11. The MOST simple description of the Internet is
    A. a single network
    B. a huge collection of different networks
    C. collection of LANs
    D. single WAN

12. How can a computer be connected to the Internet?
    A. Through internet service providers   B. Internet society
    C. Internet architecture board   D. Local area network

13. A software program that is used to view web pages is known as a(n)
    A. Internet browser   B. interpreter
    C. operating system   D. website

14. Which of the following is used to search anything on the Internet?
    A. Search engines   B. Routers
    C. Social networks   D. Websites

15. When a website is accessed, its main page is called
    A. home page   B. back end page
    C. dead end   D. both A and B

16. Google Docs provides _____, which is a salient feature of Google Doc.
    A. image processing   B. synchronization
    C. both A and B   D. installation

17. Documents in Google Drive could be accessed from
    A. only a personal computer
    B. any computer that has Internet connection
    C. only that computer that has Google drive on hard disk
    D. both B and C

18. In an email address, for example test@gmail.com, "gmail" is known as
    A. domain
    B. host computer in commercial domain
    C. internet service provider
    D. URL

19. Which of the following is NOT a well-known domain?
    A. .edu   B. .com   C. .org   D. .army

20. Cyberspace is an alternative name used for
    A. Internet   B. information   C. virtual space   D. data space

21. Which one of the following is NOT an Internet browser?
    A. Chrome   B. Firefly   C. Firefox   D. Safari

22. Which of the following is NOT a past or current search engine? 22._____
    A. Apple   B. Lycos   C. Bing   D. Google

23. Document scanning could be done through 23._____
    A. OCR   B. OMR
    C. both A and B   D. dot-matrix printer

24. _____ are used to fill out empty fields in scanned images of data. 24._____
    A. Computerized optical scanners   B. OCR software
    C. Scanners   D. Laser printers

25. All of the following are examples of hardware for standard home use EXCEPT 25._____
    A. flash drives   B. inkjet printers
    C. servers   D. laser printers

KEY (CORRECT ANSWERS)

1.	D		11.	B
2.	B		12.	A
3.	B		13.	A
4.	D		14.	A
5.	A		15.	A
6.	B		16.	B
7.	C		17.	B
8.	B		18.	B
9.	A		19.	D
10.	B		20.	A

21.	B
22.	A
23.	C
24.	A
25.	C

TEST 2

DIRECTIONS: Each question or incomplete statement is followed by several suggested answers or completions. Select the one that BEST answers the question or completes the statement. *PRINT THE LETTER OF THE CORRECT ANSWER IN THE SPACE AT THE RIGHT.*

1. In a spreadsheet, data is organized in the form of
   A. lines and spaces
   B. rows and columns
   C. layers and planes
   D. height and width

   1.____

2. Which one of the following menus is used to protect a worksheet?
   A. Edit   B. Format   C. Data   D. Tools

   2.____

3. _____ corrects spelling mistakes automatically.
   A. Word wrap
   B. AutoCorrect
   C. Spell checker
   D. Thesaurus

   3.____

4. Which function is used to automatically align text?
   A. Justification
   B. Indentation
   C. Both A and B
   D. None of the above

   4.____

5. Orientation is the property of the _____ function.
   A. Print
   B. Design
   C. Image
   D. Both A and B

   5.____

6. Special effects that are used to present slides in a presentation are known as
   A. effects
   B. custom animation
   C. transition
   D. present animation

   6.____

7. Page setup and print functions can typically be found in the ____ menu.
   A. tools   B. format   C. file   D. edit

   7.____

8. Which one of the following is considered removable storage media?
   A. Scanner
   B. Flash drive
   C. External hard drive
   D. Both B and C

   8.____

9. Which component of the computer is called the brain of the computer?
   A. ALU   B. Memory   C. Control Unit   D. CPU

   9.____

10. .txt is a file that is named for _____ files.
    A. Notepad   B. Word   C. Paint   D. Excel

    10.____

11. Software programs that are automatically downloaded and work within a browser are known as
    A. plug-in   B. utilities   C. widgets   D. add-on

    11.____

12. _____ is a computer that requests data from other computers on the Internet.
    A. Client
    B. Server
    C. Super computer
    D. Personal computer

13. A wizard is considered as a _____ file with prompt display.
    A. system   B. program   C. help   D. application

14. E-mails from unknown senders go into the _____ folder.
    A. Spam   B. Trash   C. Drafts   D. Inbox

15. LAN is an abbreviation for _____ area network.
    A. line   B. local   C. large   D. limited

16. Which of the following is NOT an extension for an image file?
    A. .bmp   B. .jpg   C. .png   D. .xls

17. In the e-mail address *test@gmail.com*, "test" is the _____ name.
    A. domain   B. user   C. server   D. ISP

18. To e-mail multiple recipients while hiding the recipients from view, use the ___ function.
    A. BCC   B. CC   C. send   D. hide

19. The system that translates an IP address into a simple form that is easy to remember is
    A. domain name system
    B. domain
    C. domain numbering system
    D. server domain

20. Which one of the following is the CORRECT method to send a file through e-mail?
    A. CC
    B. Attachment
    C. Embed through HTML
    D. Both A and B

21. Inkjet printers are categorized as a(n) _____ printer.
    A. character   B. ink   C. line   D. band

22. Which one of the following is a storage medium that has a shape of a circular plate?
    A. Disk   B. CPU   C. ALU   D. Printer

23. Ctrl+P activates the _____ function.
    A. reboot   B. save   C. print   D. paint

24. The file extension .exe represents an _____ file.
    A. examination   B. extra   C. executable   D. extension

25. Which of the following is NOT considered an input device? 25.____
    A. OCR   B. Optical scanner
    C. Printer   D. Keyboard

KEY (CORRECT ANSWERS)

1.	B		11.	B
2.	D		12.	A
3.	B		13.	C
4.	A		14.	A
5.	A		15.	B
6.	C		16.	D
7.	C		17.	B
8.	D		18.	A
9.	D		19.	A
10.	A		20.	B

21. C
22. A
23. C
24. C
25. C

TEST 3

DIRECTIONS: Each question or incomplete statement is followed by several suggested answers or completions. Select the one that BEST answers the question or completes the statement. *PRINT THE LETTER OF THE CORRECT ANSWER IN THE SPACE AT THE RIGHT.*

1. Excel is a _____ program. 1.____
   A. graphics   B. word processor
   C. spreadsheet   D. typewriter

2. Basically, a word processor program like Microsoft Word is a replacement for 2.____
   A. manual work   B. typewriters
   C. both A and B   D. graphical programs

3. Which one of the following could be added as a sound effect to a PowerPoint presentation? 3.____
   A. .wav files and .mid files   B. .wav files and .gif files
   C. .wav files and .jpg files   D. .jpg files and .gif files

4. Google Drive is an example of _____ software. 4.____
   A. system   B. application   C. database   D. firmware

5. PDF stands for _____ document format. 5.____
   A. portable   B. picture   C. plain   D. private

6. Which one of the following is an example of internal memory of a computer? 6.____
   A. Disks   B. Pen drive   C. RAM   D. CDs

7. A keyboard is an example of a(n) _____ device. 7.____
   A. input   B. output
   C. word processor   D. printing

8. Clip art is a collection of _____ that can be inserted into a document. 8.____
   A. text files   B. image files
   C. templates   D. audio files

9. _____ is a distinctive part of memory which holds the contents temporarily during cut or copy functions. 9.____
   A. Clipboard   B. Macro   C. Template   D. Clip art

10. _____ is a process to store files on a computer from the Internet. 10.____
    A. Uploading   B. Downloading
    C. Pulling   D. Transferring

11. "Cut and paste" refers to 11.____
    A. deleting and moving text   B. restoring and updating software
    C. cleaning images   D. replacing images

12. Which one of the following is a compressed format for images?
    A. GIF   B. JPGE   C. PNG   D. JPG

13. A computer stores information and data inside the
    A. hard drive   B. CPU   C. CD   D. monitor

14. WWW is an abbreviation of
    A. world wide web
    B. wide world web
    C. web worldwide
    D. world wide website

15. A _____ computer holds more than one processor.
    A. multithread
    B. multi-unit
    C. multiprocessor
    D. multiprogramming

16. Landscape and portrait are properties of
    A. page layout   B. design   C. formatting   D. text

17. _____ includes the company's name, address, phone number and e-mail address.
    A. Letterhead   B. Template   C. Visiting Card   D. Brochure

18. _____ Server provides database services for other computers.
    A. Application   B. Web   C. Database   D. FTP

19. Which one of the following is responsible for storing movies, images and pictures?
    A. File server
    B. Web server
    C. Database server
    D. Application server

20. GUI stands for graphical
    A. user interface
    B. unified instrument
    C. unified interface
    D. user instrument

21. Scanner is an example of a(n) _____ device.
    A. output   B. input   C. printing   D. both A and B

22. Which one of the following is NOT an example of computer hardware?
    A. Printer   B. Scanner   C. Mouse   D. Antivirus

23. Which one of the following provides the BEST quality reproduction of graphics?
    A. Laser printer
    B. Inkjet printer
    C. Dot-matrix printer
    D. Plotter

24. If an e-mail sender is unknown, then do not download the _____ because it might contain a virus.
    A. attachment
    B. email
    C. spam
    D. both A and B

25. The BEST way to send identical emails to more than one person is to   25._____
    A. use the CC option   B. add email ID to address
    C. forward   D. both A and B

KEY (CORRECT ANSWERS)

1.	C	11.	A
2.	B	12.	A
3.	A	13.	A
4.	B	14.	A
5.	A	15.	C
6.	C	16.	A
7.	A	17.	A
8.	B	18.	C
9.	A	19.	A
10.	B	20.	A

21. B
22. D
23. D
24. A
25. A

TEST 4

DIRECTIONS: Each question or incomplete statement is followed by several suggested answers or completions. Select the one that BEST answers the question or completes the statement. *PRINT THE LETTER OF THE CORRECT ANSWER IN THE SPACE AT THE RIGHT.*

1. A keyboard shortcut for saving files is 1.____
   A. Alt+S   B. Ctrl+S   C. Ctrl+SV   D. S+Enter

2. Which of the following is NOT a term relevant to Excel? 2.____
   A. slide   B. cell
   C. formula   D. column

3. A _____ background is a grainy and non-smooth surface. 3.____
   A. texture   B. gradient   C. solid   D. pattern

4. Word wrap forces all text to fit within the defined 4.____
   A. margin   B. indent   C. block   D. box

5. In Microsoft Word, overview of the prepared document could be better seen through 5.____
   A. Preview   B. Print Preview
   C. Review   D. both A and B

6. The amount of vertical space between text line in a document is known as 6.____
   A. double space   B. line spacing
   C. single space   D. vertical spacing

7. Which one of the following devices is required for Internet connection? 7.____
   A. Joy stick   B. Modem   C. NIC card   D. Optical drive

8. IBM is a short form used for 8.____
   A. Internal Business Management
   B. International Business Management
   C. Internal Business Machines
   D. International Business Machines

9. Which one of the following is static and non-volatile memory? 9.____
   A. RAM   B. ROM   C. BIOS   D. Cache

10. One disadvantage of Google Docs is 10.____
    A. less storage   B. compatibility
    C. needs connectivity to Internet   D. synchronization

11. WAN is an abbreviation of _____ area network. 11.____
    A. wide   B. wired   C. whole   D. while

12. Bibliography can be created through the _____ tab. 12._____
    A. References   B. Design   C. Review   D. Insert

13. The _____ is MOST likely shared in a computer network. 13._____
    A. keyboard   B. speaker   C. printer   D. scanner

14. A normal computer is not able to boot if it does not have a(n) 14._____
    A. operating system   B. complier
    C. loader   D. assembler

15. _____ is another name for junk e-mails. 15._____
    A. Spam   B. Spoof   C. Spool   D. Sniffer scripts

16. A table of contents can be created automatically by using an option in 16._____
    A. Page Layout   B. Insert   C. References   D. View

17. ALU stands for 17._____
    A. arithmetic logic unit   B. array logic unit
    C. application logic unit   D. both A and B

18. Orientation is concerned with the _____ set-up of the page. 18._____
    A. horizontal   B. vertical   C. both A and B   D. spacing

19. _____ is a form of written communication within the same company which 19._____
    comprises guide words as heading.
    A. Memorandum   B. Letterhead
    C. Template   D. None of the above

20. Which one of the following is NOT a web browser? 20._____
    A. Chrome   B. Opera   C. Firefox   D. Drupal

21. .net domain is specifically used for 21._____
    A. international organization
    B. internet infrastructure and service providers
    C. educational institutes
    D. commercial business

22. A modem is not required when the Internet is connected through 22._____
    A. Wi-Fi   B. LAN
    C. dial-up phone   D. cable

23. Mail Merge uses _____ to create separate copies of a document for 23._____
    multiple people in Microsoft Word.
    A. primary document   B. data document
    C. both A and B   D. web page

24. Linux is an example of 24._____
    A. operating system   B. malware
    C. firmware   D. application program

25. Which one of the following is a CORRECT format for a website address? 25.____
    A. www@com
    B. www.test.com
    C. www.test25A@com
    D. www#TeST.com

KEY (CORRECT ANSWERS)

1. B
2. A
3. B
4. A
5. B

6. B
7. B
8. D
9. B
10. C

11. A
12. A
13. C
14. A
15. A

16. C
17. A
18. C
19. A
20. D

21. B
22. A
23. C
24. A
25. B

EXAMINATION SECTION
TEST 1

DIRECTIONS: Each question or incomplete statement is followed by several suggested answers or completions. Select the one that BEST answers the question or completes the statement. *PRINT THE LETTER OF THE CORRECT ANSWER IN THE SPACE AT THE RIGHT.*

1. In programming, declaring a variable name involves what else other than naming?
   A. Type B. Length C. Size D. Style

   1._____

2. Name of a student is an example of
   A. operation
   C. attribute
   B. method
   D. none of the above

   2._____

3. Basic strength of a computer is
   A. speed B. memory C. accuracy D. reliability

   3._____

4. *Only girls can become members of the committee. Many of the members of the committee are officers. Some of the officers have been invited for dinner.* Based on the above statements, which is the CORRECT conclusion?
   A. All members of the committee have been invited for the dinner.
   B. Some officers are not girls.
   C. All girls are the members of the committee.
   D. None of the above

   4._____

5. Of the following statements, which of them cannot both be true and both be false?
   I. All babies cry
   III. No babies cry
   II. Some babies cry
   IV. Some babies do not cry

   The CORRECT answer is:
   A. I and II B. I and III C. III and IV D. I and IV

   5._____

6. 3, 7, 15, 31, 63, ? What number should come next?
   A. 83 B. 127 C. 122 D. 76

   6._____

7. If 30% of a number is 12.6, find the number?
   A. 45 B. 42 C. 54 D. 60

   7._____

8. 10, 25, 45, 54, 60, 75, 80. The odd one out is
   A. 10 B. 45 C. 54 D. 60

   8._____

9. Complement of an input is produced by which logical function?
   A. AND B. OR C. NOT D. XOR

   9._____

10. *If marks are greater than 70 and less than 85, then the grade is B.*
    This statement is an example of which programming control structure?
    A. Decision
    B. Loop
    C. Sequence
    D. None of the above

11. In programming, which operator is called the assignment operator?
    A. +   B. =   C. _   D. %

12. In programming, which operator is called the modulus operator?
    A. +   B. =   C. %   D. /

13. What is the correct order of running a computer program?
    A. Linking, loading, execution, translation
    B. Loading, translation, execution, linking
    C. Execution, translation, linking, loading
    D. Translation, loading, linking, execution

14. In the case of structure of programming, which of the following terms means "if none of the other statements are true"?
    A. Else   B. Default   C. While   D. If

15. True statements:
    i. All benches are chairs.
    ii. Some chairs are desks.
    iii. All desks are pillars.
    Conclusions:
    I. Some pillars are benches.
    II. Some pillars are chairs.
    III. Some desks are benches.
    IV. No pillar is a bench.

    The CORRECT answer is:
    A. None of the above
    B. Either I or IV, and III
    C. Either I or IV
    D. Either I or IV, and II
    E. All of the above

16. True statements:
    i. Some snakes are reptiles.
    ii. All reptiles are poisonous.
    iii. Some poisonous reptiles are not snakes.
    Conclusions:
    I. Some poisonous reptiles are snakes.
    II. All snakes are poisonous.
    III. All reptiles are snakes.
    IV. No poisonous reptile is a snake.

    The CORRECT answer is:
    A. None of the above
    B. Either I or IV, and III
    C. Either I or IV, and II
    D. All of the above

17. Anna runs faster than Peter.
    Jane runs faster than Anna.
    Peter runs faster than Jane.
    If the first two statements are true, the third statement would be
    A. true B. false C. unknown D. both

18. The sum of the digits of a two-digit number is 10. If the new number formed by reversing the digits is greater than the original number by 36, then what will be the original number?
    A. 37 B. 39 C. 57 D. 28

19. If an inverter is added to the output of an AND gate, what logic function is produced?
    A. AND B. NAND C. XOR D. OR

20. Decimal 7 is represented by which gray code?
    A. 0111 B. 1011 C. 0100 D. 0101

21. According to propositional logic, if p = "A car costs less than $20,000", q = "David will buy a car."
    p → ~q refers to which of the following?
    A. If David will buy a car, the car costs less than $20,000.
    B. David will not buy a car if the car costs less than $20,000.
    C. David will buy a car if the car costs less than $20,000.
    D. None of the above

22. Which Boolean algebra rule is wrong?
    A. 0 + A = A B. 0 + A = 1 C. A + A = A
    D. x • 1 = 1 E. All of the above

23. The 2's complement of 001011 is
    A. 110101 B. 010101 C. 110100 D. 010100

24. 7, 10, 8, 11, 9, 12. What number should come next?
    A. 12 B. 13 C. 8 D. 10

25. 2, 1, (1/2), (1/4). What number should come next?
    A. (1/16) B. (1/8) C. (2/8) D. 1

KEY (CORRECT ANSWERS)

1. A
2. C
3. B
4. D
5. B

6. B
7. B
8. C
9. C
10. A

11. B
12. C
13. D
14. B
15. C

16. C
17. B
18. A
19. B
20. C

21. B
22. B
23. A
24. D
25. B

TEST 2

DIRECTIONS: Each question or incomplete statement is followed by several suggested answers or completions. Select the one that BEST answers the question or completes the statement. *PRINT THE LETTER OF THE CORRECT ANSWER IN THE SPACE AT THE RIGHT.*

1. 8, 27, 64, 100, 125, 216, 343. The odd one out is
   A. 343   B. 8   C. 27   D. 100

2. In programming, what is the operator precedence?
   A. Arithmetic, comparison, logical
   B. Comparison, arithmetic, logical
   C. Arithmetic, logical, comparison
   D. Logical, arithmetic, comparison

3. Which of the following is NOT a type of programming error?
   A. Logical   B. Syntax   C. Superficial   D. Runtime

4. Statements:
   i. No man is good.   ii. Jack is a man.
   Conclusions:
   I. Jack is not good   II. All men are not Jack.

   The CORRECT answer is:
   A. I
   B. II
   C. Either I or II
   D. Neither I nor II
   E. Both I and II

5. Statements:
   i. All students are boys.   ii. No boy is dull.
   Conclusions:
   I. There are no girls in the class.   II. No student is dull.

   The CORRECT answer is:
   A. I
   B. II
   C. Either I or II
   D. Neither I nor II
   E. Both I and II

6. What is the sum of two consecutive even numbers, the difference of whose squares is 84?
   A. 32   B. 36   C. 40   D. 42

7. Choose the odd one out:

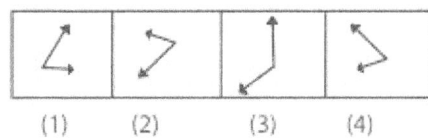

 A. 1 B. 2 C. 3 D. 4

8. In the Netherlands, almost 200 cyclists die each year on the road.
 Head injury is the main cause of death among cyclists.
 Which of the following statements is true based on the above information?
 A. In the Netherlands, if wearing a helmet was widespread among cyclists, the number of deaths in cyclists could be reduced.
 B. Too many cyclists die each year on the road in the Netherlands.
 C. Most deaths in the Netherlands occur due to cycling.
 D. None of the above

9. According to propositional logic, what is the order of precedence of operators?
 A. ^, v, ↔, →
 B. ~, ^, v, →, ↔
 C. ~, v, ^, ↔, →
 D. →, ~, ^, v, ↔

10. The binary equivalent of the number 50 is
 A. 01101 B. 11010 C. 11100 D. 110010

11. Number 200 can be represented by how many bits?
 A. 1 B. 5 C. 8 D. 10

12. Which of the following is NOT true?
 A. 0 × 0 = 0 B. 1 × 0 = 0 C. 0 × 1 = 1 D. 1 × 1 = 1

13. Get two numbers
 If first number is bigger than second then
 Print first number
 Else
 Print second number
 The above pseudo-code is an example of which control structure?
 A. Loop B. Sequence
 C. Decision D. None of the above

14. A group of variables is called
 A. data structure B. control structure
 C. data object D. linked list

15. The first character of the string variable St is represented by
 A. St[1] B. St[0]
 C. St D. none of the above

16. Statements:
    i. No girl is poor   B. All girls are rich
    Conclusions:
    I. No poor girl is rich   II. No rich girl is poor

    The CORRECT answer is:
    A. I   B. II
    C. Either I or II   D. Neither I nor II
    E. Both I and II

17. Statements:
    i. All fishes are orange in color   ii. Some fishes are heavy
    Conclusions:
    I. All heavy fishes are orange in color
    II. All light fishes are not orange in color

    The CORRECT answer is:
    A. I   B. II
    C. Either I or II   D. Neither I nor II
    E. Both I and II

18. 3, 7, 6, 5, 9, 3, 12, 1, 15. What number should come next?
    A. 18   B. 13   C. 1   D. -1

19. 5184, 1728, 576, 192. What number should come next?
    A. 64   B. 32   C. 120   D. 44

20. $(p \Leftrightarrow r) \Rightarrow (q \Leftrightarrow r)$ is equivalent to
    A. $[(\sim p \vee r) \wedge (p \vee \sim r)] \vee \sim [(\sim q \vee r) \wedge (q \vee \sim r)]$
    B. $\sim[(\sim p \vee r) \wedge (p \vee \sim r)] \vee [(\sim q \vee r) \wedge (q \vee \sim r)]$
    C. $[(\sim p \vee r) \wedge (p \vee \sim r)] \wedge [(\sim q \vee r) \wedge (q \vee \sim r)]$
    D. $[(\sim p \vee r) \wedge (p \vee \sim r)] \vee [(\sim q \vee r) \wedge (q \vee \sim r)]$

21. Which of the following propositions is a tautology?
    A. $(p \vee q) \rightarrow q$ B. $p \vee (q \rightarrow p)$ C. $p \vee (p \rightarrow q)$ D. b & c

22. According to propositional logic, if p = "Mary gets an A in computer science", q = "Mary got 90% marks in computer science."
    $p \leftrightarrow q$ refers to which of the following?
    A. Mary gets an A in computer science if and only if her percentage in computer science is 90%.
    B. Mary might get an A in computer science if her percentage in computer science is 90%
    C. Mary get an A in computer science if her percentage in computer science is 90%.
    D. None of the above

23. What does the following flowchart depict?   23._____

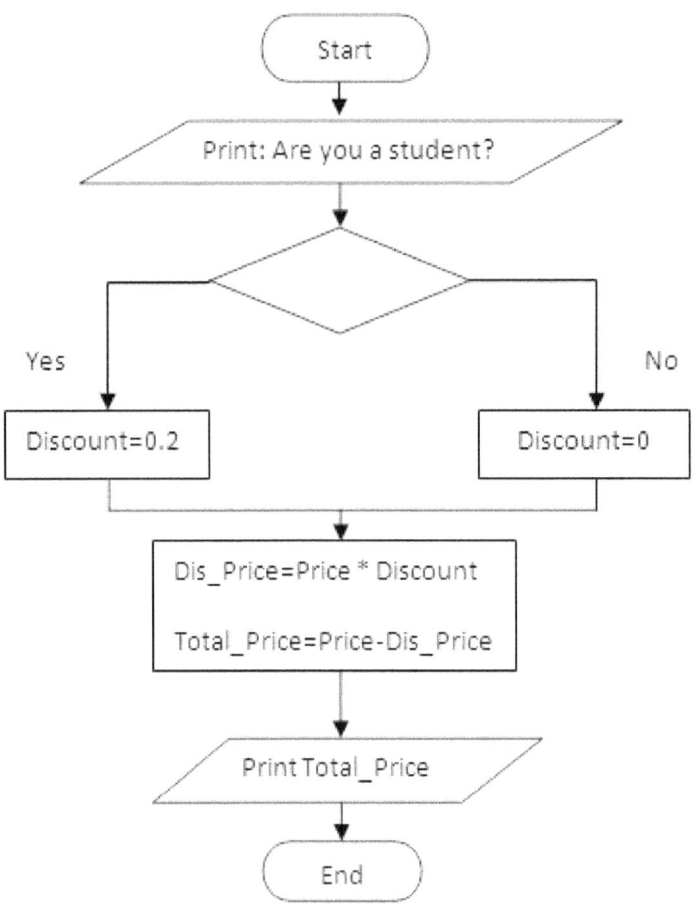

   A. All users get a discount.
   B. If user is a student, only then does he get a discount.
   C. If user is a student, he does not get a discount, while other users get a discount.
   D. None of the above

24. 13, 35, 57, 79, 911. What number should come next?   24._____
   A. 1113   B. 1114   C. 1100   D. 1111

25. Choose the missing shape.   25.____

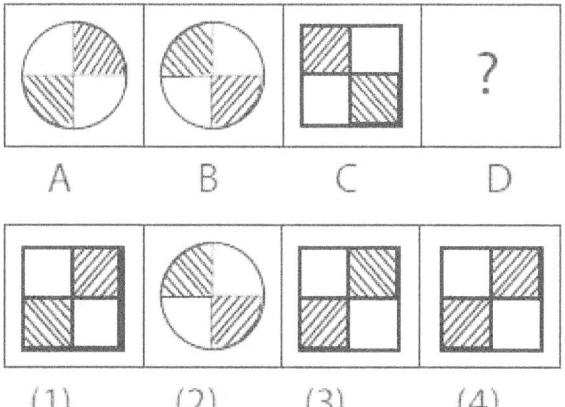

A. 1   B. 2   C. 3   D. 4

KEY (CORRECT ANSWERS)

1.	D	11.	C
2.	A	12.	C
3.	C	13.	C
4.	A	14.	A
5.	E	15.	B
6.	D	16.	E
7.	A	17.	A
8.	A	18.	D
9.	B	19.	A
10.	D	20.	B

21. D
22. A
23. B
24. C
25. C

TEST 3

DIRECTIONS: Each question or incomplete statement is followed by several suggested answers or completions. Select the one that BEST answers the question or completes the statement. *PRINT THE LETTER OF THE CORRECT ANSWER IN THE SPACE AT THE RIGHT.*

1. The following flowchart represents which control structure?   1.____

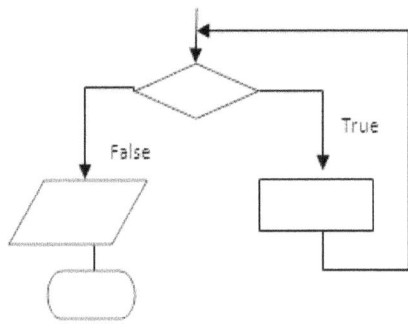

   A. If/else   B. For   C. While   D. Switch

2. The processing steps of a program are grouped into a set of related programming statements called   2.____
   A. components
   B. objects
   C. modules
   D. none of the above

3. Statements: 3.____
   i. Some engineers are intelligent
   ii. Some intelligent are poor
   Conclusions:
   I. Some engineers are poor
   II. Some poor are engineers

   The CORRECT answer is:
   A. I
   B. II
   C. Either I or II
   D. Neither I nor II
   E. Both I and II

4. Statements: 4.____
   i. No man is a fool   ii. John is a man
   Conclusions:
   I. John is not a fool   II. All men are not John

   The CORRECT answer is:
   A. I
   B. II
   C. Either I or II
   D. Neither I nor II
   E. Both I and II

5. John weighs less than Fred.
   John weighs more than Boomer.
   Of the three dogs, Boomer weighs the least.

   If the first two statements are true, the third statement is
   A. true   B. false   C. uncertain   D. both

   5.____

6. A file contains 10 sheets and none of these sheets is blue. Which of the following statements can be deduced?
   A. None of the 10 sheets contained in the file are blue.
   B. The file contains a blue sheet.
   C. The file contains at least one yellow sheet.
   D. None of the above

   6.____

7. Choose the odd one out:

   (1)   (2)   (3)   (4)

   A. 1   B. 2   C. 3   D. 4

   7.____

8. Which of the following structures requires the statements to be repeated until a condition is met?
   A. Sequence   B. If….Else
   C. For   D. None of the above

   8.____

9. While n is greater than 0
   Increment count
   end
   The above pseudo-code represents which programming structure?
   A. Sequence   B. Loop
   C. Structure   D. None of the above

   9.____

10. Which of the following converts a source code into machine code and turns it into an exe file?
    A. Linker   B. Compiler
    C. Interpreter   D. None of the above

    10.____

11. Which of the following is used to hide data and its functionality?
    A. Structure   B. Loop
    C. Object   D. Selection statement

    11.____

12. Statements:
    i. All apples are golden in color
    ii. No golden colored things are cheap
    Conclusions:
    I. All apples are cheap
    II. Golden colored apples are not cheap

    The CORRECT answer is:
    A. I
    B. II
    C. Either I or II
    D. Neither I nor II
    E. Both I and II

    12.____

13. Statements:
    i. All cups are glasses
    ii. All glasses are bowls
    iii. No bowl is a plate
    Conclusions:
    I. No cup is a plate
    II. No glass is a plate
    III. Some plates are bowls
    IV. Some cups are not glasses

    The CORRECT answer is:
    A. None of the above
    B. Either I or IV, and III
    C. Either I or IV
    D. Either I or IV, and II
    E. All of the above

    13.____

14. 331, 482, 551, 263, 383, 362, 284. The odd one out is
    A. 331   B. 383   C. 284   D. 551

    14.____

15. 3, 5, 7, 12, 17, 19. The odd one out is
    A. 7   B. 17   C. 12   D. 19

    15.____

16. Ratio of 12 minutes to 1 hour is:
    A. 2:3   B. 1:5   C. 1:6   D. 1:8

    16.____

17. 10 cats caught 10 rats in 10 seconds. How many cats are required to catch 100 rats in 100 seconds?
    A. 100   B. 50   C. 200   D. 10

    17.____

18. Four engineers and six technicians can complete a project in 8 days, while three engineers and seven technicians can complete it in 10 days. In how many days will ten technicians complete it?
    A. 40   B. 36   C. 50   D. 45

    18.____

19. According to propositional logic, if p = "Jane is smart", "q = "Jane is honest", then p v (~p ^ q) refers to which of the following?
    A. Either Jane is smart or honest.
    B. Jane is smart and honest.
    C. Either Jane is smart, or she is not smart but honest.
    D. None of the above

    19.____

20. In binary number system, the number 102 is equal to
    A. 1100110   B. 1001100   C. 1110110   D. 1100101

21. In base 8, number 362 is represented as
    A. 550   B. 552   C. 545   D. 566

22. 396, 462, 572, 427, 671, 264. The odd one out is
    A. 427   B. 572   C. 671   D. 264

23. A is two years older than B who is twice as old as C. If the total of the ages of A, B and C is 27, then how old is B?
    A. 10   B. 11   C. 12   D. 13

24. What is 50% of 40% of Rs. 3,450?
    A. 580   B. 670   C. 690   D. 570

25. What is the minimum number of colors required to fill the spaces in the following diagram without the adjacent sides having the same color?

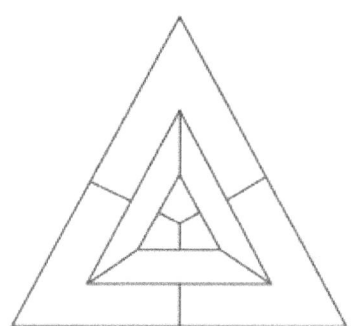

A. 3
C. 6
B. 4
D. Not possible to determine

KEY (CORRECT ANSWERS)

1. A
2. C
3. E
4. A
5. A

6. A
7. D
8. C
9. B
10. B

11. A
12. B
13. A
14. D
15. C

16. B
17. D
18. A
19. C
20. A

21. B
22. A
23. A
24. C
25. A

TEST 4

DIRECTIONS: Each question or incomplete statement is followed by several suggested answers or completions. Select the one that BEST answers the question or completes the statement. *PRINT THE LETTER OF THE CORRECT ANSWER IN THE SPACE AT THE RIGHT.*

1. Computer signals that include both measuring and counting are called 1.____
   A. analog B. digital
   C. hybrid D. none of the above

2. The result of ANDing 5 and 4 is 2.____
   A. 30 B. 9
   C. 20 D. none of the above

3. If one wants to trace an organization's purchase orders from creation to final disposition, he should use which of the following? 3.____
   A. Data flow diagram B. Internal control flow chart
   C. System flow chart D. Program flow chart

4. Statements: 4.____
   i. Some tables are sofas ii. All furniture are tables
   Conclusions:
   I. Some furniture are sofas II. Some sofas are furniture

   The two statements given should be assumed to be true. Select the conclusion.
   A. I B. II
   C. Either I or II D. Neither I nor II
   E. Both I and II

5. Statements: 5.____
   i. Many actors are singers. ii. All singers are dancers.
   Conclusions:
   I. Some actors are dancers. II. No singer is an actor.

   The CORRECT answer is:
   A. I B. II
   C. Either I or II D. Neither I nor II
   E. Both I and II

6. Anna will not pass both the verbal reasoning test and quantitative reasoning test. This statement refers to which of the following? 6.____
   A. Anna will not pass the verbal reasoning test.
   B. Anna will neither pass quantitative reasoning test nor verbal reasoning test.
   C. Anna will pass either the verbal reasoning test or the numerical reasoning test.
   D. If Anna passes the verbal reasoning test, she will not pass the numerical reasoning test.

7. Which symbol is used at the beginning of the flowchart?

    A. ◯   B. ⬭   C. ◇   D. ▭

8. A list of instructions in a proper order to solve a problem is called
    A. sequence   B. algorithm
    C. flowchart   D. none of the above

9. Statements:
    i. Some pearls are stones
    ii. Some stones are diamonds
    iii. No diamond is a gem
    Conclusions:
    I. Some gems are pearls   II. Some gems are diamonds
    III. No gem is a diamond   IV. No gem is a pearl

    The CORRECT answer is:
    A. None of the above   B. Either I or IV, and III
    C. Either I or IV   D. Either I or IV, and II
    E. All of the above

10. 53, 53, 40, 40, 27, 27. What number should come next?
    A. 14   B. 12   C. 13   D. 10

11. 1, 3, 1, 9, 1, 81, 1. What number should come next?
    A. 4   B. 1   C. 343   D. 6561

12. A father is 30 years older than his son. He will be three times as old as his son after 5 years. What is the father's present age?
    A. 30   B. 35   C. 40   D. 45

13. Ahmed is older than Ali
    Maria is older than Ahmed.
    Ali is older than Maria.
    If the first two statements are true, the third statement is
    A. true   B. false   C. unknown   D. both

14. All flowers are fruit.
    Some flowers are leaves.
    All leaves are fruit.
    If the first two statements are true, the third statement is
    A. true   B. false   C. unknown   D. both

15. The Spring Mall has more stores than the Four Seasons Mall.
    The Four Corners Mall has fewer stores than the Four Seasons Mall.
    The Spring Mall has more stores than the Four Corners Mall.
    If the first two statements are true, the third statement is
    A. true   B. false   C. unknown   D. both

3 (#4)

16. Choose the odd one out: 16.____

    A. 1   B. 2   C. 3   D. 4

17. Fact 1: All cats like to jump.   17.____
    Fact 2: Some cats like to run.
    Fact 3: Some cats look like dogs.
    If the first three statements are true, which of the following statements must also be true?
    I.   All cats who like to jump look like dogs.
    II. Cats who like to run also like to jump.
    III. Cats who like to jump do not look like dogs.

    The CORRECT answer is:
    A. I only   B. II only
    C. II and III only   D. None of the above

18. Fact 1: All chickens are birds.   18.____
    Fact 2: Some chickens are hens.
    Fact 3: Female birds lay eggs.
    If the first three statements are true, which of the following statements must also be true?
    I.   All birds lay eggs.
    II. Some hens are birds.
    III. Some chickens are not hens.

    The CORRECT answer is:
    A. I only   B. II only
    C. II and III only   D. None of the above

19. Fact 1: Jake has four watches.   19.____
    Fact 2: Two of the watches are black.
    Fact 3: One of the watches is a Rolex.
    If the first three statements are true, which of the following statements must also be true?
    I.   Jake has a Rolex.
    II. Jake has three watches.
    III. Jake's favorite color is black.

    The CORRECT answer is:
    A. I only   B. II only
    C. II and III only   D. None of the above

4 (#4)

20. Which symbol of a flowchart is used to test a condition?   20.____

   A. ◯   B. ▱   C. ◇   D. ⬭

21. Which symbol of a flowchart is used for input and output?   21.____

   A. ◯   B. ▱   C. ◇   D. ▭

22. Which of the following is NOT one of the categories of flowcharting symbols?   22.____
   A. Input/output symbols
   B. Processing symbols
   C. Storage symbols
   D. Flow symbols

23. Choose the missing shape.   23.____

   A   B   C   D

   1   2   3   4

   A. 1   B. 2   C. 3   D. 4

24. Choose the missing shape.   24.____

   A   B   C   D

   (1)   (2)   (3)   (4)

   A. 1   B. 2   C. 3   D. 4

25. How many minimum numbers of colors will be required to fill a cube without adjacent sides having the same color? 25.____
    A. 3   B. 4   C. 6   D. 8

KEY (CORRECT ANSWERS)

1. C   11. D
2. C   12. C
3. B   13. B
4. E   14. C
5. A   15. A

6. B   16. A
7. B   17. B
8. B   18. B
9. B   19. A
10. A   20. C

21. B
22. C
23. B
24. A
25. A

EXAMINATION SECTION
TEST 1

DIRECTIONS: Each question or incomplete statement is followed by several suggested answers or completions. Select the one that BEST answers the question or completes the statement. *PRINT THE LETTER OF THE CORRECT ANSWER IN THE SPACE AT THE RIGHT.*

1. _____ is the data that has been organized or presented in a meaningful fashion.   1._____
   A. A process   B. Software   C. Storage   D. Information

2. Of the following data processing functions, which one is NOT a data processing function of a computer?   2._____
   A. Data gathering   B. Processing data into information
   C. Analyzing the data or information   D. Storing the data or information

3. In electronic data processing systems, which standard data code is used commonly to represent alphabetical, numerical and punctuation characters?   3._____
   A. ASCII   B. EBCDIC   C. BCD   D. All of the above

4. Data processing performed by several separate computers/networks, at several different locations, linked by a communications facility is known as _____ processing.   4._____
   A. distributed   B. centralized   C. on-line   D. batch

5. Which process is utilized by large retailers to study market trends?   5._____
   A. Data conversion   B. Data mining
   C. Data selection   D. Pos

6. In normalization, second normal form (2NF) eliminates in Tables   6._____
   A. all hidden dependencies
   B. the possibility of insertion anomalies
   C. all non-key fields depend on the whole primary key
   D. none of the above

7. Which of the following is a bottom-up approach for database design which is designed by examining the relationship between attributes?   7._____
   A. Functional dependency   B. Normalization
   C. Decomposition   D. None of the above

8. Which is the process that is used to restore data that has been stored in a computer?   8._____
   A. Retrieve   B. Backup   C. Recovery   D. Deadlock

9. Which term BEST explains the homogenous data type?
   A. Data items of same length
   B. Data items of same type
   C. Data items of different length
   D. Numerical and character date items

10. For any category of data being processed and any type of device used for this purpose, all data processing systems perform the same steps. Which is the CORRECT sequence?
    A. Analyzing, coding and execution
    B. Input, processing and output
    C. Input, organizing and processing
    D. Processing, storage and distribution

11. Which of the following e-data processing methods works on data that is accumulated from more than location and records that are updated instantly?
    A. Minicomputer system
    B. Batch processing system
    C. On-line, real-time system
    D. Micro computer system

12. Suppose you are employed by the Air Transport Company to design a database for an airline transaction system. The database has to capture the detailed level of data related to the tickets booked by the user and the updating made by them with timestamp. Which database model would be your preference?
    A. Dimensional model
    B. It can be either dimensional model or on-line transaction processing model
    C. On-line transaction processing model
    D. None of the above

13. In the database management system, what are the after triggers functions?
    A. Triggers generated after a particular operation
    B. Triggers run after an insert, update or delete on a table
    C. Triggers run after an insert, views, update or delete on a table
    D. None of the above

14. For trigger creation, a CREATE TRIGGER statement is used. So, clause _____ specifies the table name on which the trigger is to be attached. Also, _____ specifies that it is an AFTER INSERT trigger.
    A. for insert; on
    B. on; for insert
    C. for; insert
    D. none of the above

15. Which part of a data flow diagram (DFD) represents the people and organizations that send data that the system being modeled uses or produces?
    A. Processes   B. Data source   C. Data store   D. Data flow

16. The purpose of cryptography is
    A. deadlock removal
    B. job scheduling
    C. protection
    D. file management

17. _____ memory allocation method suffers from external fragmentation.
    A. Segmentation
    B. Demand paging
    C. Swapping
    D. Paging

18. When working with a time-sharing operating system, when the time slot given to a process is completed, the process goes from the running state to the _____ state.
    A. blocked
    B. ready
    C. complete
    D. terminated

19. The purpose of real-time systems
    A. is primarily used on mainframe computers
    B. monitors events instantly as they occur
    C. is employed in program development
    D. none of the above

20. What are the causes of process termination?
    A. Process is removed from all queues and process's PCB is de-allocated
    B. Process is completed
    C. Process control block is never de-allocated
    D. None of the above

21. Fragmentation of the file system
    A. occurs only if the file system is used improperly
    B. can always be prevented
    C. can be temporarily removed by compaction
    D. is a characteristic of all file systems

22. _____ scheduling is most suitable for a time-shared interactive system. It assigns the CPU to the first process in the ready queue for q time units. After q time units, if the process is not handed over to the CPU, it is blocked, and the process is put at the tail of the ready queue (done).
    A. Shortest-job-first (SJF)
    B. CPU
    C. Round-robin (RR)
    D. None of the above

23. Backup can BEST be explained as
    A. a tool that must be offered by Windows operating system like Windows XP and 7 that checks when your system hardware and software need a new OS
    B. copy files from a computer to another medium, such as tape, DVD, another hard drive, or a removable drive
    C. a term that is used to move from one operating system to another, which may or may not involve implementing a new computer
    D. none of the above

24. As a Technical Support Officer for a large organization, at times you have to deal with login authentication problems of user computers. Which of the following is NOT a best practice for password policy?
    A. Restriction on password reuse
    B. Password encryption
    C. Having changed passwords every two years
    D. Deciding maximum age of password
    E. None of the above

24.____

25. When working in a team environment, the BEST adopted problem-solving technique in which all members of a team fully accept and support a decision is
    A. compromise   B. goal
    C. consensus   D. none of the above

25.____

KEY (CORRECT ANSWERS)

1.	D	11.	C
2.	C	12.	C
3.	A	13.	B
4.	A	14.	B
5.	B	15.	B
6.	A	16.	C
7.	B	17.	A
8.	A	18.	B
9.	B	19.	B
10.	B	20.	A

21. A
22. C
23. B
24. C
25. C

TEST 2

DIRECTIONS: Each question or incomplete statement is followed by several suggested answers or completions. Select the one that BEST answers the question or completes the statement. *PRINT THE LETTER OF THE CORRECT ANSWER IN THE SPACE AT THE RIGHT.*

1. A collection of facts like drawings, pictures and stock figures is called 1.____
   A. quantity
   B. product
   C. data
   D. collector's item
   E. information

2. The electronic data processing technique that collects data into groups to permit convenient and efficient processing is known as 2.____
   A. document-count processing
   B. batch-processing
   C. generalized-audit processing
   D. multiprogramming

3. Lee runs a grocery store; he wants to keep a record of daily sold items. Lee uses a bar chart for this purpose to show many breads he sold per day. Each day has its own bar. How could he find the total number of breads sold? 3.____
   A. Finding the height of the tallest bar
   B. Adding together the heights of all the bars in the chart
   C. Counting the number of bars
   D. Finding the average of the values of each bar

4. A summary level view of a system and the highest-level DFD is provided to the reader with the help of 4.____
   A. data store
   B. data source
   C. context diagram
   D. documentation

5. Which option BEST explains the *triggers*? 5.____
   A. A statement that enables the start of any DBMS
   B. A statement that is executed by the user when debugging an application program
   C. A statement that is executed automatically by the system as a side effect of modification to the database
   D. None of the above

6. Virtual memory technique is implemented with the help of 6.____
   A. segmentation
   B. fragmentation
   C. paging
   D. none of the above

7. Which diagram is used to represent the relationship between the input, processing and output of an AIS? 7.____
   A. Flowchart
   B. Data flow diagram
   C. Document flowchart
   D. System flowcharts

8. _____ scheduling is the simplest scheduling technique that forces the short processes to wait for very long processes.
   A. Round-robin (RR)
   B. Last-in, first out (LIFO)
   C. Shortest-job-first (SJF)
   D. First-come, first-served (FCFS)

   8._____

9. Mapping of file is managed by
   A. paging table
   B. virtual memory
   C. file system
   D. file metadata

   9._____

10. On-line analytical processing is also called _____ processing.
    A. decision support
    B. on-line transactional
    C. transaction control
    D. none of the above

    10._____

11. When working in large organizations, you have to deal with different access authentication situations. To ensure security, you have multiple options in such conditions. Which of the following is the LEAST secure method of authentication for your organization?
    A. Key card
    B. Fingerprint
    C. Retina pattern
    D. Password

    11._____

12. DML stands for
    A. data management language
    B. data markup language
    C. data manipulation language
    D. none of the above

    12._____

13. Which term BEST explains the characteristics of a computer to run several operations simultaneously?
    A. Concurrency   B. Deadlock   C. Backup   D. Recovery

    13._____

14. In DBMS, what is the BEST way to represent the attributes in a large database?
    A. Relational-and
    B. Concatenation
    C. Dot representation
    D. All of the above

    14._____

15. Database locking mechanism is used to rectify the problem of
    A. lost update
    B. uncommitted dependency
    C. inconsistent data
    D. none of the above

    15._____

16. In the scheme (dept name, size), we have relations (total inst 2010, total inst 2013). Which dependency has led to this relation?
    A. Company name, year->size
    B. Year->size
    C. Company name->size
    D. Size->year

    16._____

17. Which is the BEST possible option to evaluate any scheduling algorithm?
    A. CPU utilization
    B. Throughput
    C. Waiting time
    D. All of the above

    17._____

18. When the round robin CPU scheduling technique is adopted in a time-shared system,
    A. very large time slice degenerates into first-come, first-served algorithm
    B. extremely small time slices improve performance
    C. extremely small time slices degenerates into LIFO algorithm
    D. medium sized time slices leads to shortest request time first algorithm

    18.____

19. A priority scheduling BIGGEST issue is
    A. definite blocking   B. starvation
    C. priority queues   D. none of the above

    19.____

20.

    The above figure is called a(n) _____ in use case diagram.
    A. person   B. substitute
    C. actor (symbol)   D. flow directive

    20.____

21. Use case models can be summed up into
    A. use case diagram   B. use case description
    C. all of the above   D. none of the above

    21.____

22. Prototype
    A. is a working model of different parts at different levels or all of a final product
    B. does not represent any sort of models
    C. can never consist of full size
    D. all of the above

    22.____

23. Kim has been given some official documents to type. While typing, he notices that some of the words are automatically changing. He is very interested to understand the purpose of this feature in MS Word. AutoCorrect is designed to replace _____ words as you type.
    A. short, repetitive   B. grammatically incorrect
    C. misspelled   D. none of the above

    23.____

24. As a computer associate, you have to write different reports like weekly departmental updates and specially designed tasks to analyze the different areas of an organization. Of the following, which is considered good reporting practices?
    A. Report factual observations, not opinions
    B. Identify proper personnel
    C. Formalize your inspection criteria
    D. None of the above

    24.____

25. To improve the competency of teams, members of a(n) _____ team have been cross-trained so that each person is capable of performing the duties of all the other team members. 25._____
    A. functional
    B. cross-functional
    C. multifunctional
    D. self-directed

KEY (CORRECT ANSWERS)

1.	C	11.	D
2.	B	12.	C
3.	B	13.	A
4.	C	14.	B
5.	C	15.	C
6.	C	16.	A
7.	D	17.	D
8.	C	18.	A
9.	D	19.	B
10.	A	20.	C

21. C
22. A
23. C
24. A
25. D

TEST 3

DIRECTIONS: Each question or incomplete statement is followed by several suggested answers or completions. Select the one that BEST answers the question or completes the statement. *PRINT THE LETTER OF THE CORRECT ANSWER IN THE SPACE AT THE RIGHT.*

1. Information is _____ unfinished data.
   A. always B. not C. occasionally D. none of these

2. Which option BEST explains Beta software?
   A. An early development version of software in which there are likely to be bugs.
   B. Software will expire in 30 days after its download.
   C. Software that has successfully passed the alpha test stage.
   D. Up-gradation of software is not possible.

3. Jane drew a bar chart to show the number of different cars he saw daily on his way back home. There was no bar above the Mercedes. What does this mean?
   A. He did not see any Mercedes during his trip
   B. No Mercedes exist in his city
   C. He selected a wrong type of chart
   D. He has never seen a Mercedes before

4. A flowchart is a picture representation of a program. Flows should initiate from top to bottom and from right to left. This flowcharting principle is commonly known as the _____ rule.
   A. narrative B. sandwich C. direction D. consistency

5. The database designing approach which is based on a bottom-up approach that is designed by examining the relationship between attributes is
   A. functional dependency B. database modeling
   C. normalization D. decomposition

6. In an operating system, a situation occurs in which one process is in a waiting queue on another process that is also waiting on another process and the last one is waiting on the first process so no process is progressing in this waiting circular. This is called
   A. deadlock B. starvation
   C. dormant D. none of the above

7. Which access control method is considered the BEST approach for restricting system access to authorized users?
   A. Role-based access control B. Process-based access control
   C. Job-based access control D. None of the above

8. Which of the following is a disadvantage of a distributed system?
   A. Incremental growth B. Reliability
   C. Resource sharing D. All of the above

9. Which of the following is the BEST example of batch processing? 9.____
   A. Video game control
   B. Online reservation system
   C. Preparing pay bills of employees
   D. None of the above

10. Which of the following techniques was initiated to keep both CPU and the I/O devices busy because it was not possible with the single job? 10.____
    A. Time-sharing
    B. Spooling
    C. Preemptive scheduling
    D. Multiprogramming

11. Distributed operating system is based on the principle of 11.____
    A. single system image
    B. multi-system image
    C. wireless networks
    D. none of the above

12. The following components are helpful in a successful database environment EXCEPT 12.____
    A. users
    B. database
    C. separate files
    D. database administrator

13. In DBMS, which of the following is NOT schema? 13.____
    A. Database schema
    B. Logical schema
    C. None of the above

14. Of the following, which SQL Query is used to remove the table and all its data from the database? 14.____
    A. Drop table
    B. Delete table
    C. Alter table
    D. None of the above

15. *Ellipses* in DBMS means 15.____
    A. weak entity set
    B. attributes
    C. primary key
    D. none of the above

16. The method which performs a set of union of two "similarly structured" tables is called 16.____
    A. union
    B. join
    C. addition
    D. none of the above

17. All details about the files, its ownership, permissions, and location of file contents are stored in 17.____
    A. file control block (FCB)
    B. computer history
    C. file system
    D. none of the above

18. The drawback of a file management system to store data is 18.____
    A. data redundancy and inconstancy
    B. difficulty in accessing data
    C. data isolation
    D. all of the above

19. Which of the following is a feature of the machine independent operating system?
    A. Management of real time memory
    B. File processing
    C. I/O supervision
    D. Job scheduling
    E. B and D
    F. A and C

20. As a computer support officer, you are given details for your company's customers, consisting of two lists of names and addresses. You need to produce it in an individual document that consists of both names and address list. For this purpose, which mail merge would you prefer?
    A. Main document
    B. Data source
    C. Mail merge
    D. Merge field

21. After once creating a customer list with mail merge, which button will help you to add, delete or update your customer list?
    A. *Data Source* button
    B. *Edit* button
    C. *Edit Data Source* button
    D. *Data Editing* button

22. Which of the following steps is NOT a part of the three basic *Mail Merge Helper* steps?
    A. Merge the two files
    B. Create the main document
    C. Set the mailing list parameters
    D. Create the data source

23. As a computer support officer, while completing your assigned document typed in MS Word 2013, you need to insert the page number in the footer, but when you click on the insert tab > footer, it appears as *1*, but you wish to show *i* (roman numbers). What procedure will be followed?
    A. From Home, select bullets and numbering and configure the necessary setting
    B. From Insert Tab, choose Page Number and specify necessary setting
    C. Click on Page Number Icon and select Format Page Number and specify required setting
    D. All of the above

24. The problem statement contains the _____, which consists of these lists:
    I. Lists specific input programs
    II. Precise output values
    III. Perfect program would return for those input values

    A. Testing plan
    B. Error handler
    C. Requirement list
    D. Input-output specification

25. As a computer support officer who knows the stages of team development that will lead this team to a winning combination, what are the stages in proper sequence?
    A. Forming, storming, norming and performing
    B. Forming, norming, performing and finalizing
    C. Forming, storming, norming and playing
    D. None of the above

KEY (CORRECT ANSWERS)

1.	B		11.	B
2.	C		12.	C
3.	A		13.	B
4.	C		14.	C
5.	C		15.	B
6.	A		16.	A
7.	A		17.	A
8.	B		18.	D
9.	C		19.	E
10.	D		20.	C

21. C
22. C
23. C
24. A
25. A

TEST 4

DIRECTIONS: Each question or incomplete statement is followed by several suggested answers or completions. Select the one that BEST answers the question or completes the statement. *PRINT THE LETTER OF THE CORRECT ANSWER IN THE SPACE AT THE RIGHT.*

1. Data users are those who
   A. use data for their own advantage, breaking the law
   B. store files and data for their specific purposes
   C. use the data in databases
   D. none of the above

   1.____

2. Which type of chart would be the BEST choice for showing how the temperature of a pizza changes over time when it is put in the oven?
   A. Pie chart   B. Line graph
   C. Bar chart   D. None of the above

   2.____

3. As a computer support officer, you have to continuously update and organize your directories, folders and files on your computer. Which of the following BEST suits your requirement?
   A. Microsoft Word   B. Any spreadsheet application
   C. Windows Explorer   D. Microsoft Internet Explorer

   3.____

4. Upgrade installation means
   A. preparation for installation, installation itself, any required or optional steps following the installation
   B. completely formatting the operating system on hardware and install new software
   C. type of system installation on a computer that already has an earlier version of the operating system
   D. none of the above

   4.____

5. The main job of an operating system is
   A. command resources   B. manage resources
   C. provide utilities   D. none of the above

   5.____

6. The MOST common source of change data in refreshing a data warehouse is _____ change data.
   A. queryable   B. cooperative   C. logged   D. snapshot

   6.____

7. Which of the following is NOT an advantage of multiprogramming?
   A. Increased throughput
   B. Shorter response time
   C. Decreased operating system overhead
   D. Ability to assign priorities to jobs

   7.____

8. In ERD, the rectangles are divided into two parts that show
   A. entity set
   B. relationship set
   C. set of attributes
   D. primary key

9. The MAXIMUM numbers of entities that can be participating in a relationship are designed with
   A. minimum cardinality
   B. maximum cardinality
   C. entity relation diagram
   D. none of the above

10. Which of the following is a multi-valued attribute?
    A. Phone number
    B. Name
    C. Date of birth
    D. Place of birth
    E. None of the above

11. Which term is used to refer to a specific record in your medicine database; for instance, information stored about a specific illness?
    A. Relation
    B. Instance
    C. Table
    D. None of the above

12. The relation stud (ID, name, house no., credit, house no., city, department) is decomposed into stud1 (ID, name) stud2 (name, house no., city, department). This type of decomposition is called
    A. lossless decomposition
    B. lossless-join decomposition
    C. both A and B
    D. none of the above

13. As a technical support officer for a large organization, you have to ensure the uninterrupted availability of data by creating backup to deal with every possible data loss. Backup is taken by
    A. erasing all previous records and creating new records
    B. sending all log records from primary site to the remote backup site
    C. sending only selected records from main site to the alternate site
    D. none of the above

14. Verbal exchange of information between parents and a school staff when a student is moved from one department to another is a report which includes necessary information to maintain a consistent support for students of one department to another. This report is known as a
    A. transfer report
    B. hand-off report
    C. graphic record
    D. report

15. Which portable storage device would you prefer for backups or showing your photographs to your friend?
    A. USB stick
    B. Hard drive
    C. Joystick
    D. None of the above

16. Which is the exact step for problem solving?
    A. Observe, evaluate and adjust
    B. Collect and analyze data
    C. Identify and analyze the problem
    D. Consider possible solutions

17. The software that maintains the time of a microprocessor to assure that all time critical events are processed as efficiently as possible and also system activities are divided into independent tasks is known as
    A. shell processor
    B. kernel
    C. device driver
    D. none of the above

18. Which of the following is the MOST appropriate scheduling technique in real time operating systems?
    A. Round robin
    B. FCFS
    C. Pre-emptive scheduling
    D. Random scheduling

19. Use case diagrams consist of
    A. actor
    B. prototype
    C. none of the above
    D. all of the above

20. Data warehouse means
    A. the actual directory of a knowledge
    B. the stage of selecting the right data for a KDD process
    C. a subject-oriented integrated time variant non-volatile collection of data in support of management
    D. all of the above

21. Jane wants to advertise her home-based bakery. For this purpose she needs to develop a two-column promotion for the daily local newspaper. She selected MS Word for this purpose, but does not know exactly which option to use. Of the following, what would you suggest she use for newspaper style columns?
    A. Insert Tab > Smart Art
    B. Table > Insert Table
    C. Insert Tab > Textbox
    D. Page Layout Tab > Columns

22. Of the following, what would you suggest Jane in Question 21 use to add Shimmer and Sparkle text in her advertisement to make it more attractive and eye capturing?
    A. Word Art
    B. Font styles
    C. Text effects
    D. Font effects

23. In MS Word, which indent marker is specific to control all the lines excluding the first line?
    A. First Line Indent Marker
    B. Left Indent Marker
    C. Hanging Indent Marker
    D. Right Indent Marker

24. When working as a computer support officer, you receive a help call from one of the users. The problem is that the user has just deleted an entire folder of important office notes. He needs to retrieve the data. Which method would you adopt to retrieve the contents? 24.____
    A. Empty the recycle bin
    B. Restore the folder from the recycle bin
    C. Once deleted, its contents cannot be retrieved
    D. No need to worry. Only the folder has been deleted, not its contents.

25. Documentation can be explained as 25.____
    A. a procedure used to provide technical information to specific audiences who have specific needs for that information
    B. an explanation about all procedures and their mechanisms
    C. a method that specifies the author, source and related detail about information
    D. none of the above

KEY (CORRECT ANSWERS)

1.	B		11.	A
2.	B		12.	D
3.	C		13.	B
4.	C		14.	A
5.	B		15.	A
6.	E		16.	C
7.	C		17.	B
8.	A		18.	C
9.	B		19.	D
10.	A		20.	C

21.	D
22.	D
23.	B
24.	B
25.	C

EXAMINATION SECTION
TEST 1

DIRECTIONS: Each question or incomplete statement is followed by several suggested answers or completions. Select the one that BEST answers the question or completes the statement. *PRINT THE LETTER OF THE CORRECT ANSWER IN THE SPACE AT THE RIGHT.*

1. What is the default compressing software of Windows? 1.____
   A. WinRar
   B. 7-zip
   C. WinZip
   D. All of the above

2. Which software does NOT require special drives to run? 2.____
   A. Mouse
   B. Keyboard
   C. Joystick
   D. All of the above

3. What software is required to run PDF? 3.____
   A. MS Word
   B. Windows Media Player
   C. Adobe Photoshop
   D. Adobe Reader

4. An error message that says "there is a problem with this website's security certificate" appears when 4.____
   A. Windows is outdated
   B. browser is outdated
   C. date and time are wrong
   D. internet is disabled

5. Software should always be _____ for better performance. 5.____
   A. disabled
   B. updated
   C. uninstalled
   D. all of the above

6. SATA is the abbreviation for 6.____
   A. Sequential Advanced Technology Advancement
   B. Serial Advanced Technology Attachment
   C. Serial Automatic Technology Attachment
   D. Supper Advanced Technology Attachment

7. Which of the following is a part of management software development? 7.____
   A. People
   B. Product
   C. Process
   D. All of the above

8. _____ is a tool in the design phase. 8.____
   A. Abstraction
   B. Refinement
   C. Information Hiding
   D. All of the above

9. What is the other name used for white box software testing technique? 9.____
   A. Basic Path
   B. Graph Testing
   C. Data Flow
   D. Glass Box Testing

10. _____ is included in the Turnkey package.
    A. Software   B. Hardware
    C. Training   D. All of the above

11. _____ are types of a record access method.
    A. Sequential and random   B. Direct and immediate
    C. Sequential and indexed   D. Online and real time

12. _____ has a sequential file organization.
    A. Grocery store checkout   B. Bank checking account
    C. Payroll   D. Airline reservation

13. What will you recommend when users are involved in complex tasks?
    A. A short term memory   B. Demands on shortcut usage
    C. Both A and B   D. None of the above

14. _____ protocols are similar to HTTP.
    A. FTP; SMTP   B. FTP; SNMP
    C. FTP; MTV   D. SMTP; SNMP

15. _____ is the oldest data model.
    A. Relational   B. Deductive
    C. Physical   D. Hierarchical

16. _____ defines the transaction executed.
    A. Committed   B. Aborted
    C. Failed   D. Rolled Back

17. _____ is NOT a deadlock managing strategy.
    A. Deadlock prevention   B. Timeout
    C. Deadlock detection   D. Deadlock annihilation

18. _____ is the average execution time of the monitor power process.
    A. 1 ms   B. 10 ms
    C. 100 ms   D. None of the above

19. _____ is NOT a dimension of scalability.
    A. Size   B. Distribution
    C. Interception   D. Manageability

20. What would you do if the icons on the desktop are white or missing colors?
    A. End the explorer.exe   B. Check settings in Appearance
    C. Both A and B   D. None of the above

21. What would you do if while using AutoCAD you receive a message of "license is invalid"?
    A. Delete licensing file   B. Re-enter registration information
    C. Both A and B   D. None of the above

22. What would you do to satisfy the growing communication need in your company?
    A. Use front end processor
    B. Use a multiplexer
    C. Use a controller
    D. All of the above

23. _____ is a part of x.25.
    A. Technique for start stop data
    B. Technique for dial access
    C. DTE/DCE interface
    D. None of the above

24. Which of the following is a software product?
    A. CAD, Cam
    B. Firmware, Embedded
    C. Generic, Customized
    D. Both A and B

25. ACT in Boehm software maintenance model is the abbreviation for
    A. Actual Change Track
    B. Annual Change Track
    C. Annual Change Traffic
    D. Actual Change Traffic

KEY (CORRECT ANSWERS)

1.	C	11.	A
2.	D	12.	B
3.	D	13.	A
4.	C	14.	A
5.	B	15.	D
6.	B	16.	A
7.	D	17.	D
8.	D	18.	A
9.	D	19.	D
10.	D	20.	C

21.	C
22.	D
23.	C
24.	C
25.	C

TEST 2

DIRECTIONS: Each question or incomplete statement is followed by several suggested answers or completions. Select the one that BEST answers the question or completes the statement. *PRINT THE LETTER OF THE CORRECT ANSWER IN THE SPACE AT THE RIGHT.*

1. Software maintenance incorporates
   A. Error Correction
   B. Enhancement of capabilities
   C. Deletion of obsolete capabilities
   D. All of the above

   1.____

2. Software Maintenance model called Taute has _____ number of phases.
   A. 6   B. 7   C. 8   D. 9

   2.____

3. _____ is a software process certification.
   A. JAVA certified
   B. IBM certified
   C. ISO-9000
   D. Microsoft certified

   3.____

4. _____ is known as quality management in software development.
   A. SQA
   B. SQM
   C. SQI
   D. Both A and B

   4.____

5. Software reliability means
   A. time   B. efficiency   C. quality   D. speed

   5.____

6. A software package designed to store and manage databases is
   A. Database   B. DBMS   C. Data Model   D. Data

   6.____

7.

   The above image represents a _____ relation.
   A. many to many
   B. many to one
   C. one to one
   D. one to many

   7.____

8. The diagram shown at the right indicates that
   A. there is a missing entity
   B. students attend courses
   C. many students can attend many courses
   D. students have to attend more than one course

   8.____

9. In relational algebra, the union of two sets (set A and set B) corresponds to
   A. A OR B   B. A + B   C. A AND B   D. A - B

   9.____

10. _____ is the location of the keyboard status byte. 10._____
    A. 0040:0000H   B. 0040:0013H
    C. 0040:0015H   D. 0040:0017H

11. What is the number of maximum interrupts occurring in a PC? 11._____
    A. 64   B. 128   C. 256   D. 512

12. How many bytes are there in an operating system name in the boot block? 12._____
    A. 3   B. 5   C. 8   D. 11

13. What is the size of a DPB structure? 13._____
    A. 16   B. 32   C. 64   D. 128

14. _____ is the file system in CD. 14._____
    A. Contiguous   B. Chained   C. Indexed   D. None

15. NTFS volume is accessed directly in 15._____
    A. DOS   B. Linux   C. Windows   D. MAC

16. _____.com is an MS DOS file in the boot disk. 16._____
    A. Command   B. Start   C. Tree   D. Ver

17. _____ is a table in the OS that keeps information of files. 17._____
    A. FFT   B. FIT   C. FAT   D. DIT

18. _____ is a system programming language. 18._____
    A. C   B. PL/360
    C. PASCAL   D. All of the above

19. What would you do if the icons disappear from the Taskbar? 19._____
    A. Press Windows Key + R and type "regedit"
    B. Delete Icon stream and past icon Stream values
    C. Uncheck user interface
    D. All of the above

20. What would you do if you want to make sure the drivers of the old printers are removed? 20._____
    A. Check Server Properties   B. Check settings in Appearance
    C. Both A and B   D. None of the above

21. Microsoft has introduced _____ tool that incorporates all the automated fixes. 21._____
    A. Fix It Center   B. Fix All
    C. Fixing It   D. none of the above

22. A PC can only use one _____ device at a time. 22._____
    A. Ready Boost   B. Built-in Flash
    C. RAM   D. all of the above

23. You need to edit two registry keys called _____ if you cannot customize folders.
    A. bagMRU and Bags
    B. RAM and ROM
    C. DTE/DCE interface
    D. none of the above

24. What would you do if your PC does not have a Windows Installation disk?
    A. Select "create a system repair" disc
    B. Place a DVD in the writeable drive
    C. Create a bootable disc by the "Repair Your Computer"
    D. All of the above

25. Code of conduct defines the
    A. employees' legal and ethical obligations
    B. commitment to integrity
    C. terms and condition of the company
    D. legal contract

KEY (CORRECT ANSWERS)

1.	D	11.	C
2.	C	12.	C
3.	C	13.	B
4.	A	14.	A
5.	A	15.	A
6.	B	16.	A
7.	D	17.	A
8.	C	18.	D
9.	B	19.	D
10.	D	20.	C

21.	A
22.	A
23.	A
24.	D
25.	A

TEST 3

DIRECTIONS: Each question or incomplete statement is followed by several suggested answers or completions. Select the one that BEST answers the question or completes the statement. *PRINT THE LETTER OF THE CORRECT ANSWER IN THE SPACE AT THE RIGHT.*

1. What would you do if the drive does not open by double-clicking?
   A. Check search option in drive C
   B. Enter regsvr32/l shell32.dll in the Run
   C. Check settings in the control panel
   D. Both A and B

   1._____

2. What would you do if you attach another display unit to your PC but it remains blank?
   A. Check the cables
   B. Check display properties
   C. Select the properties to duplicate each other
   D. All of the above

   2._____

3. _____ helps you when you are locked out of Manager and Registry Editor?
   A. Virus Effect Remover   B. Fix It Tool
   C. Safe mode   D. All of the above

   3._____

4. The two types of cache memory in RAM are called
   A. ALU and CPU   B. Buffer and Procedure
   C. Date and Timing   D. DLL and STAT

   4._____

5. _____ points at the same location when the keyboard buffer is empty.
   A. Interrupt   B. Head and Tail
   C. Tail   D. All of the above

   5._____

6. _____ frequency is divided by the interval time.
   A. Output   B. Input
   C. Both A and B   D. None of the above
   E. All of the above

   6._____

7. What is the number of PPI present in a standard PC?
   A. 1   B. 4   C. 8   D. 16

   7._____

8. _____ is used as a status port of the keyboard.
   A. 64H   B. 44H
   C. 77H   D. All of the above

   8._____

9. _____ is a computer with an 80286 microprocessor.
   A. XT computer   B. PC/AT computer
   C. PS/2 computer   D. None of the above

   9._____

10. _____ is not a process.
    A. Arranging
    B. Manipulation
    C. Calculating
    D. Gathering
    10._____

11. _____ is a sequential processing application.
    A. Grades processing
    B. Payroll processing
    C. Both A and B
    D. All of the above
    11._____

12. _____ has a record disk address.
    A. Track Number
    B. Sector Number
    C. Surface Number
    D. All of the above
    12._____

13. Which printer would you NOT use while printing on a carbon form?
    A. Daisy Wheel
    B. Dot Matrix
    C. Laser
    D. None of the above
    13._____

14. A(n) _____ produces the BEST quality graphic production.
    A. laser printer
    B. inkjet printer
    C. plotter
    D. dot matrix
    14._____

15. _____ allows both read and write operations at the same time.
    A. ROM
    B. RAM
    C. EPROM
    D. None of the above
    15._____

16. _____ has the shortest access time.
    A. Cache Memory
    B. Magnetic Bubble Memory
    C. Magnetic Core Memory
    D. RAM
    16._____

17. _____ defines the status of resources assigned to the process.
    A. Process Control
    B. ALU
    C. Register Unit
    D. Process Description
    17._____

18. Memory _____ controls access to the memory.
    A. map
    B. protection
    C. management
    D. instruction
    18._____

19. _____ is able to record and track all the information in a database about animal movement once placed on the animal.
    A. POS
    B. RFID
    C. PPS
    D. GPS
    19._____

20. The print of a picture taken from a digital camera is said to be a(n)
    A. data
    B. output
    C. input
    D. none of the above
    20._____

21. _____ are the two types of record access methods.
    A. Sequential and Random
    B. Direct and Immediate
    C. Online and Real Time
    D. None of the above
    21._____

22. _____ is the most efficient method of file organization when the file is highly active.
    A. ISAM
    B. VSAM
    C. B-Tree
    D. All of the above

    22._____

23. _____ is the standard approach for storing data.
    A. MIS
    B. Structured Programming
    C. CODASYL specification
    D. None of the above

    23._____

24. Which of the following RDBMS supports client server application development?
    A. dBase V
    B. Oracle 7.1
    C. FoxPro 2.1
    D. Both A and B

    24._____

25. Which of the following techniques would you use to find the location of the element?
    A. Traversal
    B. Search
    C. Sort
    D. None of the above

    25._____

KEY (CORRECT ANSWERS)

1. D
2. D
3. A
4. B
5. B

11. C
12. D
13. C
14. C
15. B

6. B
7. B
8. A
9. B
10. D

16. A
17. D
18. A
19. B
20. B

21. A
22. A
23. C
24. B
25. B

TEST 4

DIRECTIONS: Each question or incomplete statement is followed by several suggested answers or completions. Select the one that BEST answers the question or completes the statement. *PRINT THE LETTER OF THE CORRECT ANSWER IN THE SPACE AT THE RIGHT.*

1. A band is equal to
   A. a byte
   B. a bit
   C. 100 bits
   D. none of the above

   1.____

2. The number of zeroes in each symbol in an odd-parity is
   A. odd
   B. even
   D. unknown
   D. both A and B

   2.____

3. _____ is also called an IPng.
   A. IPv4
   B. IPv5
   C. IPv6
   D. All of the above

   3.____

4. IPv6 addresses are written in
   A. hexadecimal
   B. binary
   C. decimal
   D. none of the above

   4.____

5. Green PCs are designed to
   A. minimize power consumption
   B. minimize inactive components
   C. minimize electricity bill
   D. all of the above

   5.____

6. Hyper V Network Virtualizations do not have the ability to access the outside world unless you
   A. implement a forwarding agent
   B. implement a gateway
   C. implement a CISCO NEXUS
   D. None of the above
   E. All of the above

   6.____

7. What would you do to create a shortcut of a website on the desktop?
   A. Left click on the icon present on the left side of the address bar and drag it to the desktop
   B. Save the webpage through the Save Page As
   C. Bookmark the page
   D. All of the above

   7.____

8. E-mail, word documents, web pages, video and photos are called unstructured data because
   A. they consist of text and multimedia
   B. the data cannot be stored in a database
   C. they cannot be stored in row and columns
   D. all of the above

   8.____

9. What would you do to manage corporate unstructured data?   9.____
   A. Install big data tool software
   B. Install data integration tools
   C. Install business intelligence software
   D. All of the above

10. Software-defined data center is a concept for   10.____
    A. a virtualized infrastructure
    B. fully automated control of data
    C. hardware maintenance through intelligent software
    D. all of the above

11. What is a cloud database?   11.____
    A. Internet based database provided through cloud data server
    B. Database-as-a-Service
    C. Both A and B
    D. None of the above

12. Monitor footprint refers to the   12.____
    A. disk space of your PC
    B. map of the monitor
    C. space taken up by the monitor on the desk
    D. footprints of the monitor

13. NOS are already built in   13.____
    A. UNIX   B. Mac OS
    C. Windows NT   D. Both A and B

14. _____ is an example of a network monitoring tool.   14.____
    A. Ping   B. VoIP
    C. POP3 server   D. All of the above

15. Tomato is the name of a wireless router   15.____
    A. firmware   B. WRT54GS
    C. both A and B   D. none of the above

16. _____ is a combination of software and hardware.   16.____
    A. Firmware   B. PROM
    C. EPROMs   D. All of the above

17. Object-oriented fonts are also called   17.____
    A. scalable fonts   B. vector fonts
    C. both A and B   D. screen fonts

18. What is the issue if the computer is rebooting itself?   18.____
    A. Faulty power supply   B. Faulty cooling fan
    C. Dirt on the cooling fan D. All of the above

19. What is the meaning if you receive a message "system running low on virtual memory"?
    A. The system is low on RAM
    B. The hard disc is full
    C. Both A and B
    D. None of the above

    19._____

20. Your computer freezes on startup. What is the issue?
    A. Defective hardware
    B. Faulty software
    C. Bugged OS
    D. All of the above

    20._____

21. The computer software maintenance checklist consists of
    A. update virus or install antivirus
    B. delete temporary internet file
    C. clear internet cache
    D. all of the above

    21._____

22. A CRC error is caused by
    A. a scratched DVD on disk
    B. dirt on CD/DVD
    C. partially burned CDs
    D. all of the above

    22._____

23. An error message "an invalid Windows File" means
    A. incomplete download
    B. system crash
    C. software bug
    D. all of the above

    23._____

24. What would you do if it is taking longer than usual to copy files in Windows?
    A. Install an external file such as TeraCopy
    B. Resume broken files
    C. Increase RAM
    D. Both A and B

    24._____

25. _____ software will help you protect file and folders.
    A. HideFolder
    B. Truecrypt
    C. TeraCopy
    D. None of the above

    25._____

KEY (CORRECT ANSWERS)

1. D
2. C
3. C
4. A
5. A

6. A
7. A
8. D
9. D
10. D

11. C
12. C
13. D
14. D
15. A

16. A
17. C
18. D
19. A
20. D

21. D
22. D
23. D
24. A
25. B

EXAMINATION SECTION
TEST 1

DIRECTIONS: Each question or incomplete statement is followed by several suggested answers or completions. Select the one that BEST answers the question or completes the statement. *PRINT THE LETTER OF THE CORRECT ANSWER IN THE SPACE AT THE RIGHT.*

1. A chip that is classified as *non-hermetic* will be encased in a package made from   1.____

    A. metal B. plastic C. glass D. ceramic

2. Of all the chips mounted on a computer's print board, the chip that typically breaks down LEAST often is the   2.____

    A. MPU B. RAM C. ROM D. ALU

3. The horizontal frequency range of a typical oscilloscope is   3.____

    A. 40 Hz B. 100 kHz C. 750 kHz D. 25 MHz

4. Once the computer's power supply has been identified as the source of a problem, a(n) _____ should be used to check it out.   4.____

    A. VOM
    B. current tracer
    C. capacitor
    D. frequency tracer

5. What computer component is represented by the schematic diagram symbol shown at the right?   5.____

    A. Variable resistor
    B. Transistor
    C. Diode
    D. Bridge rectifier

6. Video signals are typically traced with a(n)   6.____

    A. continuity tester
    B. VOM
    C. ordinary oscilloscope
    D. logic pulser

7. On a 6800 processor, the interrupt request line (IRQ) signal is located at pin number   7.____

    A. 4 B. D5 C. 40 D. A15

8. Which of the following devices should NEVER be attached to a computer?   8.____

    A. The ohmmeter of a VOM
    B. A multitrace oscilloscope
    C. A logic pulser
    D. An ordinary service oscilloscope

9. A soldering iron used for replacing chips should be NO higher than _____ watts.   9.____

    A. 15 B. 30 C. 60 D. 75

10. A technician uses a current tracer to test the output of a TTL chip. If the chip has a normal high output, the current flow should measure about

    A. .5 amps
    B. 40 microamps
    C. 600 microamps
    D. 1.6 milliamps

11. The purpose of a march pattern is to diagnose the computer's

    A. RAM
    B. MPU
    C. ROM
    D. I/O circuits

12. Which of the following color codes, appearing on a diode, would indicate the HIGHEST resistance value (in ohms)?

    A. Red-red-red
    B. Yellow-violet-orange
    C. Orange-orange-green
    D. Red-violet-gold

13. On a Dual In-line Package (DIP) chip, the pin number should be counted

    A. clockwise from the date code
    B. clockwise from the keyway notch
    C. counterclockwise from the date code
    D. counterclockwise from the keyway notch

14. The purpose of a PIA chip is to assist in

    A. storage
    B. synchronizing clock pulses
    C. digital/analog conversion
    D. data addressing

15. What computer component is represented by the schematic diagram symbol shown at the right?

    A. Toggle
    B. Fixed resistor
    C. Trimpot
    D. Diode

16. If a technician has performed a logic probe of the supply voltage of a bus line, the NEXT place to test is the

    A. VCC and ground pins
    B. MPU chip
    C. print board ground planes
    D. address and data pins

17. If a monitor is dead, the technician's FIRST step should be to check the

    A. green amps
    B. ac line fuse
    C. sync processors
    D. inverters

18. Which of the following test instruments is used LEAST often by computer technicians?

    A. Voltmeter
    B. Continuity tester
    C. Current tracer
    D. Logic probe

19. The program counter of a 68000 16-bit processer is a(n) _____-bit register.

    A. 8 B. 16 C. 32 D. 64

20. If a video display appears rippled or wavy, the MOST likely cause is a

    A. faulty PIA
    B. defective monitor power supply
    C. blown ac line fuse
    D. faulty VDG

21. The term *fanout* is used to describe

    A. the MPU's pulse distribution pattern
    B. the architecture of units surrounding the arithmetic logic unit
    C. the display on a VOM voltmeter
    D. how well a chip is able to drive a number of parallel loads

22. A way to INCREASE the resolution of a video monitor display is to

    A. increase the vertical sweep frequency
    B. selecting a lower bandwidth
    C. increase the horizontal sync signal coming from the video generator
    D. decrease the horizontal sweep frequency

23. If a TTL chip is examined with a VOM, a high would be any voltage that reads from

    A. −2.5V to +2.5V   B. 0V to +2.5V
    C. +2.5V to +5V   D. +3V to +10V

24. When a monitor loses its horizontal sweep, the MOST likely symptom would be

    A. *ghosting* images
    B. a bright vertical line on the screen
    C. a loss in vertical hold
    D. a folded appearance at the bottom of the screen

25. What computer component is represented by the schematic diagram symbol shown at the right?

    A. Connection
    B. Capacitor
    C. Ground
    D. Voltage regulator

KEY (CORRECT ANSWERS)

1.	B	11.	A
2.	A	12.	C
3.	B	13.	D
4.	A	14.	C
5.	A	15.	D
6.	C	16.	D
7.	A	17.	B
8.	A	18.	C
9.	B	19.	C
10.	B	20.	B

21. D
22. C
23. C
24. B
25. C

TEST 2

DIRECTIONS: Each question or incomplete statement is followed by several suggested answers or completions. Select the one that BEST answers the question or completes the statement. *PRINT THE LETTER OF THE CORRECT ANSWER IN THE SPACE AT THE RIGHT.*

1. To show up shorts and opens in a circuit, a technician would MOST likely use a(n) 1.____

   A. multitrace oscilloscope B. voltmeter
   C. continuity tester D. logic probe

2. On a 6800 processor, the reset signal is located at pin number 2.____

   A. 6 B. A12 C. 40 D. D8

3. An instruction can throw one or more _____, which in turn cause changes in different registers. 3.____

   A. stacks B. flags C. nodes D. strings

4. After a logic probe is connected, its LED reads as follows 4.____

   High   Low   Pulse

   Which of the following graphic depictions of the test signal would be a match for this reading?

   A.
   B. (High duration, Pulses)
   C.
   D. (5V / 0V)

5. A CRC run through a computer's ROM indicates a defect, but the chip proves to be good. When the indicated chip is replaced, the identical trouble is experienced. The MOST likely problem is a(n) 5.____

   A. open input circuit
   B. defective MPU
   C. short-circuited data bus
   D. faulty CRC

6. Each of the following is a difference between DIP and SMD (Surface-Mounted Device) chips EXCEPT

   A. side or sides of print board used
   B. dc/ac capacity
   C. method of mounting on print board
   D. spacing of legs

7. If a computer starts up, but then displays nothing but junk, each of the following is a possible cause EXCEPT

   A. defective CPU
   B. improperly seated boards
   C. intermittent clock failure
   D. defective video memory

8. On an 8088 processor, the read output is located at pin number

   A. 29   B. D6   C. 32   D. 40

9. A video display appears folded over on the bottom, with a whitish haze appearing. The MOST likely cause for this is

   A. too much vertical sweep
   B. defective monitor power supply
   C. loss of horizontal sweep
   D. PIA chip defect

10. What computer component is represented by the schematic diagram symbol shown at the right?

    A. Crystal
    B. Inductor
    C. Fuse
    D. Integrated circuit

11. How many control lines are there from the PIA chip to the Video Display Generator?

    A. 2   B. 5   C. 10   D. 17

12. Which of the following instruments is used MOST often during the examination of digital circuits?

    A. Logic probe   B. Voltmeter
    C. Current tracer   D. Frequency counter

13. When a computer stops dead, the technician's FIRST step should be to check the

    A. power supply   B. MPU
    C. RAM   D. data bus lines

14. How many address-type registers are included in a 68000 16-bit processor?

    A. 2   B. 7   C. 18   D. 32

Questions 15-17.

DIRECTIONS: Questions 15 through 17 refer to the figure below, a cross-sectional diagram of a field-effective transistor (FET). Place the letter that corresponds to each diagrammed signal in the space at the right.

15. Gate 15._____

16. Drain 16._____

17. Source 17._____

18. To read the digital voltages of a circuit, a technician should use a(n) 18._____

    A. VOM   B. logic probe
    C. ohmmeter   D. regular duty oscilloscope

19. What computer component is represented by the schematic diagram symbol shown at the right? 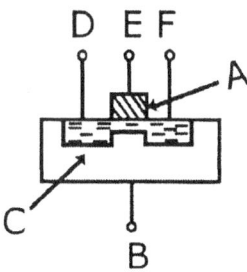 19._____

    A. Capacitor
    B. Bridge rectifier
    C. LED
    D. Transformer

20. The BEST way to examine a SAM chip that takes over the address bus is by 20._____

    A. a board check with a current tracer
    B. a pin-by-pin check with a continuity tester
    C. replacement of the chip
    D. a pin-by-pin check with a logic probe

21. The MAIN *disadvantage* associated with DIP chips is that they 21._____

    A. need both sides of the print board to be attached
    B. require four-sided leg mounting
    C. have pins that protrude out the bottom of the chip
    D. have legs spaced inconveniently close together

22. Which of the following would be LEAST likely to respond in static tests with a Substitution Machine? 22._____

    A. Regular RAM   B. ROM
    C. I/O chips   D. Dynamic RAM

23. If a CMOS chip is examined with a VOM, a *low* voltage reading would be any voltage that reads lower than

    A. -2.5V   B. 0.8   C. 1.8V   D. 4.2V

24. Which of the following color codes, appearing on a diode, would indicate the LOWEST resistance value (ohms)?

    A. Blue-gray-red
    B. Red-violet-gold
    C. Orange-white-yellow
    D. Blue-blue-green

25. Each of the following is a likely cause for an open circuit EXCEPT

    A. cold solder joint
    B. splashed solder
    C. faulty IC socket
    D. broken connector wire

KEY (CORRECT ANSWERS)

1.	C	11.	B
2.	C	12.	A
3.	B	13.	A
4.	C	14.	B
5.	C	15.	E
6.	B	16.	F
7.	C	17.	D
8.	C	18.	A
9.	A	19.	C
10.	A	20.	D

21. A
22. D
23. C
24. B
25. B

EXAMINATION SECTION
TEST 1

DIRECTIONS: Each question or incomplete statement is followed by several suggested answers or completions. Select the one that BEST answers the question or completes the statement. *PRINT THE LETTER OF THE CORRECT ANSWER IN THE SPACE AT THE RIGHT.*

1. A track and a sector number on a disk combine to form a(n)

    A. register   B. byte   C. address   D. file name

2. A(n) _____ microcomputer system design focuses on what must be done, but not on how to do it.

    A. logical   B. listed   C. protocol   D. objective

3. An instruction is retrieved from main memory by the _____ processor component.

    A. arithmetic and logic unit   B. instruction counter
    C. register   D. instruction control unit

4. What is the term for a support program that reads a source program, translates the source statements to machine language, and outputs a complete binary object program?

    A. Scheduler   B. Interpreter   C. Compiler   D. Assembler

5. A(n) _____ is composed of a group of related data records.

    A. array   B. list   C. directory   D. file

6. What is the term for an extra bit added to data bits that will allow a computer to check the bit pattern for accuracy?

    A. End code   B. Bit stuffer
    C. Operand   D. Parity bit

7. When disks are stacked into a pack, what is the term for the set of tracks accessed by the access device?

    A. Block   B. Sector   C. Cylinder   D. Drum

8. Any data communications medium can be described by the generic term

    A. line   B. port   C. converter   D. modem

9. The operating systems of most microcomputers are driven by

    A. commands   B. hardware
    C. software   D. a control unit

10. What is the term for a complete machine-level program that is in a form ready to be placed into main memory and executed?

    A. Load module   B. Object module
    C. Schedule   D. Compiler

11. A programmer writes one instruction for each machine-level instruction when using a(n)

    A. generator B. assembler
    C. resource fork D. compiler

12. A binary digit is represented by a

    A. byte B. code C. bit D. buffer

13. Which module of the operating system is responsible for communicating with input and output devices?

    A. Command processor B. Boot
    C. IOCS D. Bus line

14. Two or more disks stacked on a common drive shaft are known as a

    A. pack B. roll-out
    C. multidrive D. cylinder

15. The _____ of an operating system loads programs into main memory.

    A. compiler B. processor manager
    C. scheduler D. assembler

16. A _____ can be used to synchronize devices or media that operate at different speeds.

    A. buffer B. spooler C. modem D. protocol

17. The part of an instruction that identifies memory locations to participate in an operation is the

    A. pulse B. statement
    C. operand D. operation code

18. What is the term for a support program that reads a single source statement, translates the statement to machine language, executes the instructions, and then moves onto the next source statement?

    A. Scheduler B. Interpreter
    C. Compiler D. Assembler

19. _____ is used to link a computer's internal components.

    A. Cables B. Bus lines
    C. Clock pulses D. Motherboard

20. Data are transferred from main memory to a disk's surface in units called

    A. sectors B. blocks C. tracks D. words

21. Under a _____ memory management scheme, programs are stored on disk, with only active portions stored into memory.

    A. virtual B. dynamic
    C. block-oriented D. fixed partition

22. A(n) _____ is composed of a group of related data fields.

    A. array   B. list   C. record   D. file

23. Which of the following serves to allocate a processor's time?

    A. User
    C. Operating system
    B. Bus
    D. Motherboard

24. On a disk, the address of the beginning of each program is stored on the

    A. tree   B. block   C. index   D. register

25. A program's steps are divided into units of

    A. code
    C. sectors
    B. commands
    D. instructions

KEY (CORRECT ANSWERS)

1. C
2. A
3. D
4. C
5. D

6. D
7. C
8. A
9. A
10. A

11. B
12. C
13. C
14. A
15. C

16. A
17. C
18. B
19. B
20. A

21. A
22. C
23. C
24. C
25. D

TEST 2

DIRECTIONS: Each question or incomplete statement is followed by several suggested answers or completions. Select the one that BEST answers the question or completes the statement. *PRINT THE LETTER OF THE CORRECT ANSWER IN THE SPACE AT THE RIGHT.*

1. The address of the next instruction to be executed is held in the _____ processor component.

    A. main memory
    B. register
    C. arithmetic and logic unit
    D. instruction control unit

2. What is the term for an electronic signal that is part of a protocol?

    A. Token   B. Reach   C. Chord   D. Pulse

3. Under _____ processing, data records are processed in the order in which they are recorded.

    A. continuous   B. consecutive
    C. serial   D. sequential

4. _____ processing is a computer application in which data are collected over time and then processed together.

    A. Transaction   B. Cumulative
    C. Batch   D. Continuous

5. A(n) _____ serves as a hardware/software interface.

    A. buffer   B. application
    C. operating system   D. bus

6. Any connection for an electronic communication line can be called a(n)

    A. port   B. poll   C. line   D. front end

7. During a single machine cycle, a processor retrieves and executes

    A. one command
    B. one instruction
    C. at least two statements
    D. at least two instructions

8. A _____ is NOT an example of a data structure.

    A. record   B. file   C. list   D. directory

9. Which of the following serves to translate a computer's internal codes and a peripheral device's external codes?

    A. Buffer   B. RAM
    C. Interface   D. Encoder/decoder

74

10. Which of the following is the memory management scheme MOST often used with time-shared systems?

    A. Pages
    B. Roll-in/roll-out
    C. Fixed partitions
    D. First-come/first-serve

11. When the same data are recorded in two or more files, _____ has occurred.

    A. redundancy
    B. leakage
    C. backup
    D. loss

12. For a batch processing application, a _____ file organization should be selected.

    A. sequential
    B. indexed
    C. direct
    D. random

13. If a bus line transmits bits one by one, it is described as a _____ line.

    A. serial
    B. consecutive
    C. continuous
    D. parallel

14. Data is converted from analog to digital form through the process of

    A. demodulation
    B. data flow
    C. cross-modulation
    D. modulation

15. A _____ loads a computer's operating system.

    A. program loader
    B. IOCS
    C. command processor
    D. boot

16. Which of the following differentiates a computer from a calculator?

    A. Memory
    B. Input
    C. A processor
    D. A stored program

17. Which element of a microcomputer system will devote a separate unit to suit each peripheral?

    A. Bus
    B. Channel
    C. Motherboard
    D. Interface

18. What is the term for the interference that distorts electronic signals transmitted over a distance?

    A. Ghosting
    B. Noise
    C. Static
    D. Interference

19. By responding to a(n) _____, an operating system can switch from program to program.

    A. operand
    B. user
    C. interrupter
    D. program

20. If a microcomputer system's memory capacity is adjusted, the result will be a change in

    A. word size
    B. processing speed
    C. precision
    D. seek time

21. A _____ generates the regular electronic pulses that drive a computer. 21.___

    A. clock   B. IOCS   C. bus   D. processor

22. Under what type of access can data records be accessed in any order? 22.___

    A. Serial   B. Random
    C. Direct   D. Sequential

23. A _____ is a brief message printed or displayed by a program or the operating system that asks the user for input. 23.___

    A. token   B. seek   C. protocol   D. prompt

24. Data on a disk are recorded in a series of concentric circles called 24.___

    A. blocks   B. tracks   C. cycles   D. sectors

25. What is the term for a programming language in which one mnemonic source statement is coded for each machine-level instruction? 25.___

    A. Scheduler   B. Interpreter
    C. Compiler   D. Assembler

KEY (CORRECT ANSWERS)

1. B   11. A
2. A   12. A
3. D   13. A
4. C   14. D
5. C   15. D

6. A   16. D
7. B   17. D
8. D   18. B
9. C   19. C
10. B   20. B

21. A
22. C
23. D
24. B
25. D

EXAMINATION SECTION
TEST 1

DIRECTIONS: Each question or incomplete statement is followed by several suggested answers or completions. Select the one that BEST answers the question or completes the statement. *PRINT THE LETTER OF THE CORRECT ANSWER IN THE SPACE AT THE RIGHT.*

1. Each of the following is a problem in long-distance data transmissions that can be overcome by converting the digital signals to analog signals EXCEPT

    A. higher power requirements
    B. attenuation
    C. repeater loss
    D. introduction of spurious signals

2. The two primary determinants of data transmission speed are

    A. bandwidth and media
    B. baud and bandwidth
    C. baud and distance
    D. distance and media

3. The last record on a sequential file is known as a(n)

    A. trailer label
    B. link
    C. end message
    D. stop bit

4. Which of the following transmission media does NOT offer analog transmission?

    A. Twisted-pair wire
    B. Coaxial cable
    C. Microwave
    D. Optical fiber

5. Parallel bit transmission requires AT LEAST _____ wires.

    A. 2   B. 5   C. 8   D. 16

6. Which of the following *AT* modem commands is used to reset the modem's registers?

    A. +++   B. R   C. Z   D. Reg

7. Data transmissions can be classified as each of the following EXCEPT

    A. baseband
    B. ultraspectrum
    C. broadband
    D. voiceband

8. A communications device which sends a message and then requires switching in order to receive a message is described as

    A. simplex
    B. duplex
    C. half-duplex
    D. multiplex

9. What is the common range (miles) of a typical microwave signal?

    A. 10   B. 25   C. 40   D. 80

10. Each location on a computer network is called a

    A. node   B. station   C. sector   D. terminal

11. Each of the following is an advantage associated with using synchronous data transmission EXCEPT

    A. ability to compress data
    B. fast throughput due to bit flow
    C. rapid demodulation of signals
    D. ability to address terminals directly using address codes in the frames

12. According to the X.25 standard, a PDN packet must ALWAYS contain _____ bits.

    A. 16   B. 84   C. 128   D. 248

13. The back-end processor in a hierarchical network handles

    A. input/output   B. data processing
    C. security tasks   D. data communication

14. The purpose of a CRC is to

    A. check the accuracy of a transferred file
    B. extract stop bits during data compression
    C. provide an interface during computer-to-computer communications
    D. convert a simplex device into duplex

15. The measure of signal changes in a communications channel per second is known as

    A. skip   B. baud
    C. noise   D. bandwidth

16. Each of the following is a disadvantage associated with parallel bit transmission EXCEPT

    A. cable costs
    B. relatively low transmission speed
    C. incompatibility with some public carriers
    D. differing arrival times for transmitted bits

17. What is the term for the amount of data processing work a computer can perform in a given amount of time?

    A. Capacity   B. Threshold
    C. Thrashing   D. Throughput

18. Which of the following *AT* modem commands is used to repeat a previously given command?

    A. A/   B. &   C. X   D. RR

19. If a PC has both a COMM1 port and an internal modem, which of the following steps must be taken FIRST during IRQ conflict resolution?

    A. Set the internal modem to COMM1
    B. Disabling the modem
    C. Set the COMM1 port to COMM2
    D. Disabling the COMM1 port

20. When the computers in a ring network are interconnected, a _____ network is created. 20.____

 A. mesh
 B. star
 C. bus
 D. token ring

21. Which of the following file transfer protocols uses small packets of 128 bits? 21.____

 A. XMODEM   B. YMODEM   C. ZMODEM   D. Kermit

22. Which of the following is NOT a use associated with wide area networks? 22.____

 A. Centralizing file information
 B. Remote data entry
 C. Interoffice voice communications
 D. Time sharing

23. A network in which each piece of computer equipment can only communicate with its adjacent neighbors is termed a 23.____

 A. mesh
 B. star
 C. private branch exchange
 D. ring

24. Which of the following transmission media typically offers the GREATEST maximum data rate? 24.____

 A. Twisted-pair wire
 B. Coaxial cable
 C. Optical fiber
 D. Microwave

25. Each of the following is a purpose of a terminal program EXCEPT 25.____

 A. automating connection process
 B. processing error bits in a transmission
 C. transferring files between two computers
 D. controlling modem setup

KEY (CORRECT ANSWERS)

1.	B	11.	C
2.	B	12.	C
3.	A	13.	B
4.	D	14.	A
5.	C	15.	B
6.	C	16.	B
7.	B	17.	D
8.	C	18.	A
9.	C	19.	D
10.	A	20.	A

21. A
22. C
23. D
24. D
25. B

TEST 2

DIRECTIONS: Each question or incomplete statement is followed by several suggested answers or completions. Select the one that BEST answers the question or completes the statement. *PRINT THE LETTER OF THE CORRECT ANSWER IN THE SPACE AT THE RIGHT.*

1. Which of the following *AT* modem commands is used to turn the speaker off? 1.____

   A. M   B. &W   C. -   D. #

2. What is the term for a data communications device that allows several users to share communication channels? 2.____

   A. Star
   B. Multiplexer
   C. Distributor
   D. Token ring

3. Which of the following is NOT typically a component of a synchronous message frame? 3.____

   A. An 8-bit error code
   B. A 16-bit device address
   C. Two repetitive start characters, each 8 bits long
   D. A message number

4. Which of the following steps in the file transfer process would be performed LAST? 4.____

   A. Select protocol for distant end
   B. Notify distant end of file to be transferred
   C. Select protocol for user end
   D. Notify term program of file to be transferred

5. Which of the following is a *line of sight* transmission medium? 5.____

   A. Microwave
   B. Optical fiber
   C. Radio wave
   D. Coaxial cable

6. Most of a network's operations are backed up and stored on 6.____

   A. floppy disks
   B. the server's hard disk
   C. external hard disks
   D. magnetic tape

7. Each of the following is an advantage commonly associated with asynchronous data transmission EXCEPT 7.____

   A. relatively inexpensive equipment requirements
   B. no need for synchronized clocks
   C. transmission of each character can occur independently over a wire
   D. easy adaptation to bus networks

8. The MOST common setting between PCs connected by modem is 8.____

   A. Parity, 6 data bits, 2 stop bits
   B. No parity, 7 data bits, 1 stop bit
   C. No parity, 8 data bits, 1 stop bit
   D. Parity, 8 data bits, 2 stop bits

9. Which of the following *AT* modem commands is used to pause an operation?

   A. +++   B. *   C. ,   D. P

10. Which of the following file transfer protocols is slow, tout good for transferring files over noisy telephone lines?

    A. XMODEM   B. YMODEM   C. ZMODEM   D. Kermit

11. When empty and filled message frames are relayed from one device in a network to another, _____ occurs.

    A. capturing
    B. branch exchange
    C. token passing
    D. looping

12. The purpose of IRQ is to

    A. control input and output
    B. provide security to the server
    C. interpret parallel transmissions
    D. convert analog signals

13. The MAIN disadvantage associated with synchronous data transmission is

    A. dependence on accuracy of timing clocks to interpret signals
    B. frequent interference by spurious signals
    C. difficulty in processing error codes
    D. rapid signal degradation

14. Which of the following file transfer protocols is considered the BEST and MOST sophisticated?

    A. XMODEM   B. YMODEM   C. ZMODEM   D. Kermit

15. The *distant end* in a network is the

    A. server
    B. back-end processor
    C. node farthest from the server
    D. answering modem

16. What is the term for the process of temporarily storing input or output data on an intermediary storage medium?

    A. Capturing
    B. Spooling
    C. Holding
    D. Buffing

17. What type of computer network allows for simultaneous voice and data communications?

    A. Bus network
    B. Computer branch exchange
    C. Star network
    D. Private branch exchange

18. The simultaneous transmission of bits along several wires is known as _____ transmission.

    A. wide-area   B. serial   C. analog   D. parallel

19. What is the term for the practice of computers on a bus network to check whether a channel is free before transmitting data?

    A. Contention protocol B. Multiplexing
    C. Token passing D. Branch exchange

    19.____

20. What type of data transmission specifically uses one or more *start bits* for each eight-bit string of data?

    A. Analog B. Asynchronous
    C. Synchronous D. Digital

    20.____

21. Which of the following *AT* modem commands is used to dial the phone number that follows a command?

    A. P B. D C. @ D. AT

    21.____

22. Typically, which of the following steps in the file transfer process would be performed FIRST?

    A. Select protocol for distant end
    B. Notify distant end of file to be transferred
    C. Select protocol for user end
    D. Notify term program of file to be transferred

    22.____

23. Which of the following file transfer protocols is equipped with the BEST error checking and correction capability?

    A. XMODEM B. YMODEM
    C. YMODEM BATCH D. Kermit

    23.____

24. Without the use of devices such as repeaters, which of the following transmission media typically has the SHORTEST range?

    A. Analog twisted-pair wire
    B. Microwave
    C. Analog coaxial cable
    D. Digital coaxial cable

    24.____

25. The MAIN disadvantage associated with asynchronous data transmission is that it

    A. permits only point-to-point transmissions
    B. requires several timed clock pulses
    C. is sometimes too slow to be useful
    D. needs a separate modulator and demodulator

    25.____

KEY (CORRECT ANSWERS)

1.	A	11.	C
2.	B	12.	A
3.	A	13.	A
4.	C	14.	C
5.	A	15.	D
6.	D	16.	B
7.	D	17.	B
8.	C	18.	D
9.	C	19.	A
10.	D	20.	B

21. B
22. B
23. D
24. C
25. A

EXAMINATION SECTION
TEST 1

DIRECTIONS: Each question or incomplete statement is followed by several suggested answers or completions. Select the one that BEST answers the question or completes the statement. *PRINT THE LETTER OF THE CORRECT ANSWER IN THE SPACE AT THE RIGHT.*

1. Physical components of computers are known as 1.____
   A. software   B. hardware   C. firmware   D. human ware

2. A touchscreen is considered a(n) _____ device. 2.____
   A. input   B. output   C. display   D. both A and B

3. Keyboards and microphones are examples of computer 3.____
   A. peripherals   B. software   C. add-ons   D. uploads

4. Unauthorized access to a computer is prevented through the use of 4.____
   A. passwords   B. user logins
   C. access control software   D. computer keys

5. In order to establish an Internet connection, a modem is always connected to a 5.____
   A. keyboard   B. monitor
   C. telephone line   D. printer

6. _____ does NOT hold data permanently. 6.____
   A. RAM   B. ROM   C. Hard drive   D. Flash drive

7. Identification of a user who comes back to the same website is done through the use of 7.____
   A. scripts   B. plug-in   C. cookies   D. both A and B

8. File _____ is the process of moving a file from one computer to another computer across the network. 8.____
   A. encryption   B. transfer   C. copying   D. updating

9. _____ is a type of software that controls specific hardware. 9.____
   A. Driver   B. Browser   C. Plug-in   D. Control panel

10. _____ is a downloadable program that is used for Internet surfing. 10.____
    A. Messenger   B. Firefox
    C. Windows Explorer   D. Internet

11. In Microsoft Word, _____ is NOT a font style. 11.____
    A. Bold   B. Regular   C. Superscript   D. Italic

85

12. Which of the following is NOT associated with page margins in a Word document?
    A. Top   B. Center   C. Left   D. Right

13. Microsoft Office is a type of _____ software.
    A. application   B. system   C. Internet   D. website

14. A function that is inside another function is known as a(n) _____ function.
    A. round   B. nested   C. sum   D. average

15. To write a formula in Microsoft Excel, a user would start by typing
    A. %   B. =   C. #   D. @

16. The individual boxes used for data entry in an Excel file are known as
    A. cells
    B. data points
    C. formulas
    D. squares

17. In PowerPoint, _____ do NOT show with the slide layout.
    A. titles   B. animations   C. lists   D. charts

18. _____ is a basic option when looking for colorful images or graphics to publish in a PowerPoint presentation.
    A. Clip art
    B. Online search
    C. MS Paint
    D. Drawing

19. In a web browser, the addresses of Internet pages are known as
    A. web pages   B. URLs   C. scripts   D. plug-in

20. A company that provides Internet services is called a(n)
    A. ISP   B. IBM   C. LAN   D. Both A and B

21. _____ is the process of copying a file from personal computer to a remote computer.
    A. Downloading
    B. Uploading
    C. Updating
    D. Modification

22. _____ is a text that opens another page when clicked.
    A. Link
    B. Hyperlink
    C. Both A and B
    D. Web page

23. Dots per inch is the measure of printing
    A. quality   B. type   C. time   D. layout

24. _____ is the collection of computers connected with each other.
    A. Group   B. Team   C. Network   D. Meeting

25. Which one of the following is considered a high-end printer?
    A. Dot matrix printer
    B. Inkjet printer
    C. Laser
    D. Thermal

KEY (CORRECT ANSWERS)

1. B
2. D
3. A
4. A
5. C

6. A
7. C
8. B
9. A
10. B

11. C
12. B
13. A
14. B
15. B

16. A
17. B
18. A
19. B
20. A

21. B
22. C
23. A
24. C
25. C

TEST 2

DIRECTIONS: Each question or incomplete statement is followed by several suggested answers or completions. Select the one that BEST answers the question or completes the statement. *PRINT THE LETTER OF THE CORRECT ANSWER IN THE SPACE AT THE RIGHT.*

1. Which one of the following is a storage device? 1.____
   A. Printer B. Hard drive
   C. Scanner D. Motherboard

2. DVD is an example of a(n) _____ disk. 2.____
   A. hard B. optical C. magnetic D. floppy

3. _____ computers provide resources to other computers across the network. 3.____
   A. Server B. Client C. Framework D. Digital

4. Random access memory is considered _____ computer memory. 4.____
   A. non-volatile B. volatile C. cache D. permanent

5. Which one of the following is NOT an operating system? 5.____
   A. Windows B. IOS C. Android D. MS Office

6. A(n) _____ is a person who gets illegal access to a computer system and steals information. 6.____
   A. administrator B. computer operator
   C. hacker D. programmer

7. Which one of the following is NOT application software? 7.____
   A. MS Word B. Media player
   C. Linux D. MS Power Point

8. Which one of the following represents a domain name? 8.____
   A. .com B. www C. URL D. HTTP

9. _____ is NOT an example of an Internet browser. 9.____
   A. Opera B. Google
   C. Mozilla D. Internet Explorer

10. Which one of the following is/was NOT a search engine? 10.____
    A. Altavista B. Bing
    C. Yahoo D. Facebook

11. E-mail is an abbreviation of 11.____
    A. electronic mail B. easy mail
    C. electric email D. both A and B

12. A(n) _____ is a person who takes care of websites for large companies.
    A. administrator B. webmaster
    C. programmer D. hacker

13. _____ connect web pages with each other.
    A. Connecters B. Links C. Hyperlinks D. Browsers

14. _____ is a program that is harmful for computers.
    A. Spam B. Virus
    C. Operating system D. Plug-in

15. CC is an abbreviation of _____ in emails.
    A. core copy B. copycat
    C. carbon copy D. copy copy

16. Software most commonly used for basic personal computing is
    A. Excel B. SPSS C. Illustrator D. Dreamweaver

17. _____ is an option to send the same letter to different persons.
    A. Template B. Macros C. Mail Merge D. Layout

18. Which one of the following is a file extension for MS Word?
    A. .doc B. .txt C. .bmp D. .pdf

19. _____ displays the number of words in a document.
    A. Character Count B. Word Count C. Word Wrap D. Thesaurus

20. In an Excel sheet, an active cell is specified with
    A. dotted border B. dark wide border
    C. italic text D. a dotted border

21. A(n) _____ is a file that contains rows and columns.
    A. database B. spreadsheet
    C. word D. drawing

22. _____ are objects on the slides that hold text in a PowerPoint presentation.
    A. Placeholders B. Text holders
    C. Auto layouts D. Object holders

23. Which one of the following brings up the first slide in a PowerPoint presentation?
    A. Ctrl+End B. Ctrl+Home
    C. Page up D. Next slide button

24. Which one of the following sends printing commands to a printer?
    A. F5 B. Ctrl+P C. Ctrl+S D. F12

25. Scanners are used to capture _____ copy of documents.
    A. soft B. hard C. single D. first

KEY (CORRECT ANSWERS)

1. B
2. B
3. A
4. B
5. D

6. C
7. C
8. A
9. B
10. D

11. A
12. B
13. C
14. B
15. C

16. A
17. C
18. A
19. B
20. B

21. B
22. A
23. B
24. B
25. B

TEST 3

DIRECTIONS: Each question or incomplete statement is followed by several suggested answers or completions. Select the one that BEST answers the question or completes the statement. *PRINT THE LETTER OF THE CORRECT ANSWER IN THE SPACE AT THE RIGHT.*

1. Which one of the following is the MOST appropriate operation to move a text block in MS Word?
   A. Cut
   B. Save As
   C. Cut and Paste
   D. Copy and Paste

   1.____

2. The Navigation pane opens under the _____ tab.
   A. View
   B. Review
   C. Page Layout
   D. Mailings

   2.____

3. Ctrl+B makes selected test
   A. italic
   B. bold
   C. bigger
   D. uppercase

   3.____

4. _____ is NOT an acceptable formula in Excel.
   A. 10+50
   B. =10+50
   C. =B7+B8
   D. =B7*B8

   4.____

5. A worksheet usually contains _____ columns.
   A. 128
   B. 256
   C. 512
   D. 320

   5.____

6. _____ is the process of getting data from the cell that is located in different worksheets.
   A. Accessing
   B. Referencing
   C. Updating
   D. Functioning

   6.____

7. The shortcut _____ selects all PowerPoint slides at once.
   A. Ctrl+Home
   B. Ctrl+A
   C. Alt+Home
   D. Shift+A

   7.____

8. By pressing Ctrl+V in a Word document, the user
   A. pastes text
   B. cuts and pastes text
   C. adds a video box
   D. deletes a page

   8.____

9. Transitions are applicable only on
   A. Excel worksheets
   B. PowerPoint slides
   C. image files
   D. Word document

   9.____

10. In MS Word, the _____ tab has options for margin, orientation and spacing.
    A. Design
    B. Review
    C. Page Layout
    D. Insert

    10.____

11. Which one of the following is graphic software?
    A. MS Office
    B. Adobe Photoshop
    C. Firefox
    D. Notepad

    11.____

12. Which one of the following is a social networking website?
    A. Facebook
    B. Yahoo
    C. Google
    D. ASK

    12.____

13. A computer monitor is referred to as a(n) _____ device.
    A. output   B. input   C. sound   D. printing

14. _____ memory is another name for the main memory of the computer.
    A. Primary   B. Direct   C. Simple   D. Quick

15. An operating system is _____ software.
    A. application   B. system   C. editing   D. both A and C

16. Which one of the following pieces of equipment is necessary for video calls?
    A. Webcam   B. Mouse   C. Scanner   D. Printer

17. _____ is a primary input device that is used to enter text and numbers.
    A. Mouse   B. Keyboard   C. Joystick   D. Microphone

18. Of the following, which is NOT an example of a web browser?
    A. Firefox   B. Opera   C. Chrome   D. Google Talk

19. A _____ is a collection of many web pages that are related to each other.
    A. web browser   B. website
    C. search engine   D. Firefox

20. Which one of the following is considered a personal journal used for posts?
    A. Blog   B. E-mail   C. Chat   D. Messengers

21. Windows _____ provides security against external threats.
    A. antivirus   B. spyware   C. firmware   D. firewall

22. Desktop and laptop computers are different from each other in terms of _____ and cost.
    A. operating system   B. functions
    C. physical structure   D. application software

23. _____ is a process of stealing confidential information without permission of the user.
    A. Forwarding B. Hacking   C. Searching   D. Complaining

24. RAM is located in the _____ board.
    A. extension   B. external   C. mother   D. chip

25. All files on the computer are stored in
    A. hard drive   B. RAM
    C. cache   D. associative memory

KEY (CORRECT ANSWERS)

1. C
2. A
3. B
4. A
5. B

6. B
7. B
8. A
9. B
10. C

11. B
12. A
13. A
14. A
15. B

16. A
17. B
18. D
19. B
20. A

21. D
22. C
23. B
24. C
25. A

TEST 4

DIRECTIONS: Each question or incomplete statement is followed by several suggested answers or completions. Select the one that BEST answers the question or completes the statement. *PRINT THE LETTER OF THE CORRECT ANSWER IN THE SPACE AT THE RIGHT.*

1. Which one of the following functions are performed by RAM? 1.____
   A. Read and Write B. Read
   C. Write D. Update

2. _____ is an example of secondary storage. 2.____
   A. Diode B. Hard disk C. RAM D. ROM

3. USB is a type of _____ storage. 3.____
   A. primary B. secondary C. tertiary D. temporary

4. MPG file extension is used for _____ files. 4.____
   A. video B. audio C. image D. flash

5. .exe is an extension for _____ files. 5.____
   A. saved B. executable C. system D. software

6. Which one of the following is NOT a type of printer? 6.____
   A. Inkjet B. Dot matrix C. Laser D. CRT

7. _____ sends digital data across a phone line. 7.____
   A. Flash B. Modem C. NIC card D. Keyboard

8. _____ is a wireless technology used to transfer data among devices over short distances. 8.____
   A. USB B. Modem C. Wi-Fi D. Bluetooth

9. A user is listening to a song on his computer's music player. He is most likely listening to a(n) _____ file. 9.____
   A. .exe B. .mus C. .wav D. .mp3

10. PNG is an extension used for _____ files. 10.____
    A. audio B. video C. text D. image

11. Cache memory is located in the 11.____
    A. monitor B. CPU C. DVD D. hard drive

12. Computer resolution determines the number of 12.____
    A. colors B. pixels C. images D. icons

13. _____ is an extension used for images. 13.____
    A. GIF B. MP3 C. MPG D. PPT

14. Which one of the following is NOT an e-mail server? 14.____
    A. Gmail   B. Yahoo   C. Chrome   D. Hotmail

15. _____ is an operating system developed by Apple. 15.____
    A. Mac IOS   B. Linux   C. Android   D. Windows

16. "What You See Is What You Get" (WYSIWYG) refers to 16.____
    A. editing text and graphics for web design
    B. buying a computer at a set price that can't be negotiated
    C. purchasing products as is on websites like Amazon and eBay
    D. printing web pages exactly as they appear on the screen

17. Which one of the following is the BEST option to add a new slide in an existing PowerPoint presentation? 17.____
    A. File, add a new slide   B. File, open
    C. Insert, new slide   D. File, new

18. _____ is the default setup for page orientation in PowerPoint. 18.____
    A. Horizontal   B. Vertical   C. Landscape   D. Portrait

19. Items in a list are typically shown by using 19.____
    A. graphics   B. bullets   C. icons   D. markers

20. In PowerPoint, _____ displays only text. 20.____
    A. outline view   B. slide show
    C. print view   D. slider sorter view

21. In Excel, a cell can be edited by use of 21.____
    A. a single click   B. a double click
    C. the format menu   D. formulas

22. Formulas are important features of Microsoft 22.____
    A. Word   B. PowerPoint   C. Excel   D. Publisher

23. In MS Word, which one of the following is used to underline a text? 23.____
    A. Ctrl+I   B. Ctrl+B   C. Ctrl+U   D. Ctrl+P

24. Page color option can be found under the _____ tab. 24.____
    A. Page Layout   B. Design   C. Insert   D. View

25. The F1 key typically displays a program's ____ menu. 25.____
    A. print   B. help
    C. tools   D. task manager

KEY (CORRECT ANSWERS)

1.	A	11.	B
2.	B	12.	B
3.	C	13.	A
4.	A	14.	C
5.	B	15.	A
6.	D	16.	A
7.	B	17.	C
8.	D	18.	C
9.	D	19.	B
10.	D	20.	A

21. A
22. C
23. C
24. B
25. B

READING COMPREHENSION
UNDERSTANDING AND INTERPRETING WRITTEN MATERIAL

EXAMINATION SECTION
TEST 1

DIRECTIONS: Each question or incomplete statement is followed by several suggested answers or completions. Select the one that BEST answers the question or completes the statement. *PRINT THE LETTER OF THE CORRECT ANSWER IN THE SPACE AT THE RIGHT.*

Questions 1-7.

DIRECTIONS: Questions 1 through 7 are to be answered SOLELY on the basis of the following passage.

The first step in establishing a programming development schedule is to rate the programs to be developed or to be maintained on the basis of complexity, size, and input-output complexity. The most experienced programmer should rate the program complexity based on the system flow chart. The same person should do all of the rating so that all programs are rated in the same manner. If possible, the same person who rates the complexity should estimate the program size based on the number of pages of coding. This rating can easily be checked, after coding has been completed, against the number of pages of coding actually produced. If there is consistent error in the estimates for program size, all future estimates should be corrected for this error or the estimating method reviewed.

The input-output rating is a mechanical count of the number of input and output units or tapes which the program uses. The objective is to measure the number of distinct files which the program must control.

After the ratings have been completed, the man-days required for each of the tasks can be calculated. Good judgment or, if available, a table of past experience is used to translate the ratings into man-days, the units in which the schedule is expressed. The calculations should keep the values for each task completely separate so that a later evaluation can be made by program, programmer, and function.

After the values have been calculated, it is a simple matter to establish a development schedule. This can be a simple bar chart which assigns work to specific programmers, a complex computer program using the *PERT* technique of critical path scheduling, or other useful type of document.

1. The rating and estimating of the programs should be performed by

   A. the person who will do the programming
   B. a programmer trainee
   C. the most experienced programmer
   D. the operations supervisor

2. The measurement used to express the programming schedule is the number of

   A. distinct files controlled by the programmer
   B. man-days
   C. pages of coding
   D. programmers

3. A mechanical count of the number of input and output units or tapes should be considered as a(n)

   A. input-output rating
   B. measure of the number of man-days required
   C. rating of complexity
   D. estimate of the number of pages of coding

4. Programming development scheduling methods are for

   A. new programs only
   B. programs to be developed and maintained
   C. large and complicated programs only
   D. maintenance programs only

5. If there is a consistent error in the estimates for program size, all estimates should be

   A. adjusted for future programs
   B. eliminated for all programs
   C. replaced by rating of complexity
   D. replaced by input-output rating

6. It is intimated that

   A. the calculations should keep the valuations for each task completely separated
   B. it is a simple matter to establish a development schedule
   C. the man-days required for each of the tasks can be calculated
   D. a later evaluation will be made

7. Complexity of programs can be checked

   A. before coding has been completed
   B. after future estimates have been corrected for error
   C. as a first step in establishing a complex computer program
   D. with reference to the number of pages of coding produced

Questions 8-13.

DIRECTIONS: Questions 8 through 13 are to be answered SOLELY on the basis of the following passage.

The purposes of program testing are to determine that the program has been coded correctly, that the coding matches the logical design, and that the logical design matches the basic requirements of the job as set down in the specifications. Program errors fall into the following categories: errors in logic, clerical errors, misidentification of the computer components' functions, misinterpretation of the requirements of the job, and system analysis errors.

The number of errors in a program will average one for each 125 instructions, assuming that the programmer has been reasonably careful in his coding system. The number of permutations and combinations of conditions in a program may reach into the billions before each possibility has been thoroughly checked out. It is, therefore, a practical impossibility to check out each and every possible combination of conditions—the effort would take years, even in the simplest program. As a result, it is quite possible for errors to remain latent for a number of years, suddenly appearing when a particular combination is reached which had not previously occurred.

Latent program errors will remain in operating programs, and their occurrence should be minimized by complete and thorough testing. The fact that the program is operative and reaches end-of-job satisfactorily does not mean that all of the exception conditions and their permutations and combinations have been tested. Quite the contrary, many programs reach end-of-job after very few tests, since the *straight-line* part of the program is often simplest. However, the exceptions programmed to deal with a minimal percentage of the input account for a large percentage of the instructions. It is, therefore, quite possible to reach the end-of-job halt with only 10% of the program checked out.

8. One of the MAIN points of this passage is that

   A. it is impossible to do a good job of programming
   B. reaching end-of-job means only 10% of the program is checked out
   C. standard testing procedures should require testing of every possible combination of conditions
   D. elimination of all errors can never be assured, but the occurrence of errors can be minimized by thorough testing

9. Latent program errors GENERALLY

   A. evade detection for some time
   B. are detected in the last test run
   C. test the number of permutations and combinations in a program
   D. allow the program to go to end-of-job

10. Which one of the following statements pertaining to errors in a program is CORRECT?

    A. If the program has run to a normal completion, then all program errors have been eliminated.
    B. Program errors, if not caught in testing, will surely be detected in the first hundred runs of the program.
    C. It is practically impossible to verify that the typical program is free of errors.
    D. A program that is coded correctly is free of errors.

11. Among other things, program testing is designed to

    A. assure that the documentation is correct
    B. assure that the coding is correct
    C. determine the program running time
    D. measure programmer's performance

12. The difficulty in detecting errors in programs is due to　　　　　　　　　　　　　　　　　　12.____

    A. the extremely large number of conditions that exist in a program
    B. poor analysis of work errors
    C. very sophisticated and clever programming
    D. reaching the end-of-job halt with only 10% of the program checked out

13. If the program being tested finally reaches the end-of-job halt, it means that　　　　　　13.____

    A. one path through the program has been successfully tested
    B. less than 10% of the program has been tested
    C. the program has been coded correctly
    D. the logical design is correct

Questions 14-20.

DIRECTIONS: Questions 14 through 20 are to be answered SOLELY on the basis of the following passage.

Systems analysis represents a major link in the chain of translations from the problem to its machine solution. After the problem and its requirements for solution have been stated in clear terms, the systems analyst defines the broad outlines of the machine solution. He must know the overall capabilities of the equipment, and he must be familiar with the application. The ultimate output of the analysis is a detailed job specification containing all the tools necessary to produce a series of computer programs. The purpose of the specifications is to document and describe the system by defining the problem and the proposed solution, explain system outputs and functions, state system requirements for programmers, and to avoid misunderstandings among involved departments. The specification serves as a link between the analysis of the problem and the next function, programming. Systems analysis relies on creativity rather than rote analysis to develop effective computer systems. But this creativity must be channeled and documented effectively if lasting value is to be obtained.

14. According to the above paragraph, the systems analyst MUST be familiar with　　　　　14.____

    A. programming and the machine solution
    B. the machine solution and the next function
    C. the application and programming
    D. the application and the equipment capabilities

15. According to the above paragraph, the time that systems analysis MUST be performed is　15.____

    A. *after* the problem analysis
    B. *after* programming
    C. *before* problem definition
    D. *before* problem analysis

16. According to the above paragraph, the MAIN task performed by the systems analyst is to　16.____

    A. write the program
    B. analyze the problem
    C. define the overall capacities of the equipment
    D. define the machine solution of the problem

17. According to the above paragraph, the document produced by the systems analyst as his main output does NOT normally include

   A. an explanation of system outputs
   B. system requirements for programmers
   C. a statement of the problem
   D. performance standards

17.____

18. According to the above paragraph, the systems analysis function is

   A. relatively straightforward, requiring little creative effort
   B. extremely complex, making standard procedures impossible
   C. primarily a rote memory procedure
   D. a creative effort

18.____

19. According to the above paragraph, the specification

   A. is a major link in the sequence from problem to machine solution
   B. states the problem and its requirements for solution
   C. is chiefly concerned with the overall capabilities of the equipment
   D. represents the ultimate product of systems analysis

19.____

20. According to the above paragraph, the sequential function after the analysis of the program is

   A. documentation   B. application
   C. definition   D. programming

20.____

Questions 21-25.

DIRECTIONS: Questions 21 through 25 are to be answered SOLELY on the basis of the following passage.

Currently, memory represents one of the main limitations on computer performance and, as a result, is one of the areas where technological improvements will prove most fruitful.

Historically, the main problem of computer memories has been a very unfavorable cost-to-speed ratio. Memory devices which have great speed cost disproportionately more than those with less speed. This problem has forced computer designers to use minimum amounts of rapid access memory and to rely mainly on slower, large capacity storage. This practice has resulted in a *memory tree,* where a hierarchy of memory devices provides various increments of storage at different costs and speeds for various purposes.

To achieve better speed/cost ratios, designers are increasingly turning to memory media other than the traditional ferrite cores. These cores now account for over 90% of the memory market. Plated wire and semiconductors are the media most likely to supplant ferrite cores. Semiconductors are expected to rapidly displace cores, starting with higher speed memories. Their costs are dropping sharply and are expected to drop as much as five-fold by the middle of this decade, while their speeds are at least doubling.

Despite the increasing use of competing technologies, ferrite cores will probably still dominate the extended random access storage area. Since the largest increment of storage is associated with ferrite core memory devices, their share of the internal memory market was well over 50% by 1980. The only factor militating against this is the possibility that the largest manufacturers of computers may abandon the extended internal storage concept.

Memory developments likely to happen later in this decade include the progressive replacement of magnetic drums by magnetic disks. The latter were themselves displaced near the end of the seventies by electro optical units, followed by magnetic bubble storage. It also may prove possible to show the feasibility of associative processors. Under this concept, which is still experimental, data access would be considerably speeded through use of Contents-Addressable-Memories (CAM).

21. According to the above passage, a hierarchy of memory devices which provides various increments of storage at different costs and speeds has been used by designers because

    A. one of the larger manufacturers of computers might abandon the extended internal storage concept
    B. of the very unfavorable cost-to-speed ratio of computer memories
    C. magnetic disks have progressively replaced magnetic drums in the mid-seventies
    D. data access is expected to be appreciably speeded up through the use of Content-Addressable-Memories

22. According to the above passage, which of the following memory developments is MOST likely to have occurred by 1980?

    A. Designers will turn to memories other than core for 90% of their needs.
    B. Cores and semiconductors will largely replace plated wire memories.
    C. Cores and semiconductors will largely be replaced by electro optical and magnetic bubble storage.
    D. Ferrite core will continue to dominate the internal memory market.

23. According to the above passage, the speed/cost ratio for semiconductors is

    A. becoming more favorable
    B. the same as the speed/cost ratio for plated wire
    C. remaining constant
    D. less favorable than the speed/cost ratio for ferrite core

24. According to the information in the passage, development of improved memory technology is IMPORTANT because

    A. it demonstrates the feasibility of associative processors
    B. memory represents one of the chief limitations on computer performance today
    C. semiconductors are expected to largely replace core which now represents about half of the memory market
    D. data can now be speeded through the use of CAM

25. Three types of memory media which are discussed in the above passage are

    A. core, plated wire, semiconductors
    B. high speed buffer, magnetic disks, rotating magnetic storage
    C. ferrite cores, magnetic drums, remote data terminals
    D. high speed buffers, magnetic disks, magnetic drums

KEY (CORRECT ANSWERS)

1.	C	11.	B
2.	B	12.	A
3.	A	13.	A
4.	B	14.	D
5.	A	15.	A
6.	D	16.	D
7.	D	17.	D
8.	D	18.	D
9.	A	19.	D
10.	C	20.	D

21. B
22. D
23. A
24. B
25. A

TEST 2

DIRECTIONS: Each question or incomplete statement is followed by several suggested answers or completions. Select the one that BEST answers the question or completes the statement. *PRINT THE LETTER OF THE CORRECT ANSWER IN THE SPACE AT THE RIGHT.*

Questions 1-5.

DIRECTIONS: Questions 1 through 5 are to be answered SOLELY on the basis of the following paragraph.

Work standards presuppose an ability to measure work. Measurement in office management is needed for several reasons. First, it is necessary to evaluate the overall efficiency of the office itself. It is then essential to measure the efficiency of each particular section or unit and that of the individual worker. To plan and control the work of sections and units, one must have measurement. A program of measurement goes hand in hand with a program of standards. One can have measurement without standards, but one cannot have work standards without measurement. Providing data on amount of work done and time expended, measurement does not deal with the amount of energy expended by an individual although, in many cases, such energy may be in direct proportion to work output. Usually from two-thirds to three-fourths of all work can be measured. However, less than two-thirds of all work is actually measured because measurement difficulties are encountered when office work is non-repetitive and irregular, or when it is primarily mental rather than manual. These obstacles are often used as excuses for non-measurement far more frequently than is justified.

1. According to the above paragraph, an office manager cannot set work standards unless he can

    A. plan the amount of work to be done
    B. control the amount of work that is done
    C. estimate accurately the quantity of work done
    D. delegate the amount of work to be done to efficient workers

1._____

2. According to the above paragraph, the type of office work that would be MOST difficult to measure would be

    A. checking warrants for accuracy of information
    B. recording payroll changes
    C. processing applications
    D. making up a new system of giving out supplies

2._____

3. According to the above paragraph, the ACTUAL amount of work that is measured is _____ of all work.

    A. less than two-thirds
    B. two-thirds to three-fourths
    C. less than three-sixths
    D. more than three-fourths

3._____

4. Which of the following would be MOST difficult to determine by using measurement techniques?

    A. The amount of work that is accomplished during a certain period of time
    B. The amount of work that should be planned for a period of time
    C. How much time is needed to do a certain task
    D. The amount of incentive a person must have to do his job

4._____

5. The one of the following which is the MOST suitable title for the above paragraph is   5.____

   A. HOW MEASUREMENT OF OFFICE EFFICIENCY DEPENDS ON WORK STANDARDS
   B. USING MEASUREMENT FOR OFFICE MANAGEMENT AND EFFICIENCY
   C. WORK STANDARDS AND THE EFFICIENCY OF THE OFFICE WORKER
   D. MANAGING THE OFFICE USING MEASURED WORK STANDARDS

Questions 6-9.

DIRECTIONS: Questions 6 through 9 are to be answered SOLELY on the basis of the following passage.

Work measurement concerns accomplishment or productivity. It has to do with results; it does not deal with the amount of energy used up, although in many cases this may be in direct proportion to the work output. Work measurement not only helps a manager to distribute work loads fairly, but it also enables him to define work success in actual units, evaluate employee performance, and determine where corrective help is needed. Work measurement is accomplished by measuring the amount produced, measuring the time spent to produce it, and relating the two. To illustrate, it is common to speak of so many orders processed within a given time. The number of orders processed becomes meaningful when related to the amount of time taken.

Much of the work in an office can be measured fairly accurately and inexpensively. The extent of work measurement possible in any given case will depend upon the particular type of office tasks performed, but usually from two-thirds to three-fourths of all work in an office can be measured. It is true that difficulty in work measurement is encountered, for example, when the office work is irregular and not repeated often, or when the work is primarily mental rather than manual. These are problems, but they are used as excuses for doing no work measurement far more frequently than is justified.

6. According to the above passage, which of the following BEST illustrates the type of information obtained as a result of work measurement?   6.____

   A. Clerk takes one hour to file 150 folders
   B. Typist types five letters
   C. Stenographer works harder typing from shorthand notes than she does typing from a typed draft
   D. Clerk keeps track of employees' time by computing sick leave, annual leave, and overtime leave

7. The above passage does NOT indicate that work measurement can be used to help a supervisor to determine   7.____

   A. *why* an employee is performing poorly on the job
   B. *who* are the fast and slow workers in the unit
   C. *how* the work in the unit should be divided up
   D. *how* long it should take to perform a certain task

8. According to the above passage, the kind of work that would be MOST difficult to measure would be such work as   8.____

A. sorting mail
B. designing a form for a new procedure
C. photocopying various materials
D. answering inquiries with form letters

9. The excuses mentioned in the above passage for failure to perform work measurement can be BEST summarized as the

    A. repetitive nature of office work
    B. costs involved in carrying out accurate work measurement
    C. inability to properly use the results obtained from work measurement
    D. difficulty involved in measuring certain types of work

Questions 10-13.

DIRECTIONS: Questions 10 through 13 are to be answered SOLELY on the basis of the following passage.

Job analysis combined with performance appraisal is an excellent method of determining training needs of individuals. The steps in this method are to determine the specific duties of the job, to evaluate the adequacy with which the employee performs each of these duties, and finally to determine what significant improvements can be made by training.

The list of duties can be obtained in a number of ways: asking the employee, asking the supervisor, observing the employee, etc. Adequacy of performance can be estimated by the employee, but the supervisor's evaluation must also be obtained. This evaluation will usually be based on observation.

What does the supervisor observe? The employee, while he is working; the employee's work relationships; the ease, speed, and sureness of the employee's actions; the way he applies himself to the job; the accuracy and amount of completed work, its conformity with established procedures and standards; the appearance of the work; the soundness of judgment it shows; and, finally, signs of good or poor communication, understanding, and cooperation among employees.

Such observation is a normal and inseparable part of the everyday job of supervision. Systematically recorded, evaluated, and summarized, it highlights both general and individual training needs.

10. According to the above passage, job analysis may be used by the supervisor in

    A. increasing his own understanding of tasks performed in his unit
    B. increasing efficiency of communication within the organization
    C. assisting personnel experts in the classification of positions
    D. determining in which areas an employee needs more instruction

11. According to the above passage, the FIRST step in determining the training needs of employees is to

    A. locate the significant improvements that can be made by training
    B. determine the specific duties required in a job
    C. evaluate the employee's performance
    D. motivate the employee to want to improve himself

12. On the basis of the above passage, which of the following is the BEST way for a supervisor to determine the adequacy of employee performance?   12.____

    A. Check the accuracy and amount of completed work
    B. Ask the training officer
    C. Observe all aspects of the employee's work
    D. Obtain the employee's own estimate

13. Which of the following is NOT mentioned by the above passage as a factor to be taken into consideration in judging the adequacy of employee performance?   13.____

    A. Accuracy of completed work
    B. Appearance of completed work
    C. Cooperation among employees
    D. Attitude of the employee toward his supervisor

Questions 14-15.

DIRECTIONS: Questions 14 and 15 are to be answered SOLELY on the basis of the following paragraph.

The fundamental characteristic of the type of remote control which management needs to bridge the gap between itself and actual operations is the more effective use of records and reports – more specifically, the gathering and interpretation of the facts contained in records and reports. Facts, for management purposes, are those data (narrative and quantitative) which express in simple terms the current standing of the agency's program, work, and resources in relation to the plans and policies formulated by management. They are those facts or measures (1) which permit management to compare current status with past performance and with its forecasts for the immediate future, and (2) which provide management with a reliable basis for long-range forecasting.

14. For management purposes, facts are, according to the above paragraph,   14.____

    A. forecasts which can be compared to current status
    B. data which can be used for certain control purposes
    C. a fundamental characteristic of a type of remote control
    D. the data contained in records and reports

15. An inference which can be drawn from this statement is that   15.____

    A. management which has a reliable basis for long-range forecasting has at its disposal a type of remote control which is needed to bridge the gap between itself and actual operations
    B. data which do not express in simple terms the current standing of the agency's program, work, and resources in relationship to the plans and policies formulated by management may still be facts for management purposes
    C. data which express relationships among the agency's program, work, and resources are management facts
    D. the gap between management and actual operations can only be bridged by characteristics which are fundamentally a type of remote control

Questions 16-17.

DIRECTIONS: Questions 16 and 17 are to be answered SOLELY on the basis of the following passage.

Two approaches are available in developing criteria for the evaluation of plans. One approach, designated Approach A, is a review and analysis of characteristics that differentiate successful plans from unsuccessful plans. These criteria are descriptive in nature and serve as a checklist against which the plan under consideration may be judged. These characteristics have been observed by many different students of planning, and there is considerable agreement concerning the characteristics necessary for a plan to be successful.

A second approach to the development of criteria for judging plans, designated Approach B, is the determination of the degree to which the plan under consideration is economic. The word *economic* is used here in its broadest sense; i.e., effective in its utilization of resources. In order to determine the economic worth of a plan, it is necessary to use a technique that permits the description of any plan in economic terms and to utilize this technique to the extent that it becomes a *way of thinking* about plans.

16. According to Approach B, the MOST successful plan is *generally* one which   16._____

    A. costs least to implement
    B. gives most value for resources expended
    C. uses the least expensive resources
    D. utilizes the greatest number of resources

17. According to Approach A, a successful plan is one which is   17._____

    A. descriptive in nature
    B. lowest in cost
    C. similar to other successful plans
    D. agreed upon by many students of planning

Questions 18-20.

DIRECTIONS: Questions 18 through 20 are to be answered SOLELY on the basis of the following passage.

The primary purpose of control reports is to supply information intended to serve as the basis for corrective action if needed. At the same time, the significance of control reports must be kept in proper perspective. Control reports are only a part of the planning-management information system. Control information includes nonfinancial as well as financial data that measure performance and isolate variances from standard. Control information also provides feedback so that planning information may be updated and corrected. Whenever possible, control reports should be designed so that they provide feedback for the planning process as well as provide information of immediate value to the control process.

Since the culmination of the control process is the taking of necessary corrective action to bring performance in line with standards, it follows that control information must be directed to the person who is organizationally responsible for taking the required action. Usually the same information, though in a somewhat abbreviated form, is given to the responsible manager's superior. A district sales manager needs a complete daily record of the performance of each of his salesmen; yet, the report forwarded to the regional sales manager summarizes only the performance of each sales district in his region. In preparing reports for higher echelons of management, summary statements and recommendations for action should appear on the first page; substantiating data, usually the information presented to the person directly responsible for the operation, may be included if needed.

18. A control report serves its primary purpose as part of the process which leads DIRECTLY to

    A. better planning for future action
    B. increasing the performance of district salesmen
    C. the establishment of proper performance standards
    D. taking corrective action when performance is poor

19. The one of the following which would be the BEST description of a control report is that a control report is a form of

    A. planning   B. communication
    C. direction   D. organization

20. If control reports are to be effective, the one of the following which is LEAST essential to the effectiveness of control reporting is a system of

    A. communication   B. standards
    C. authority   D. work simplification

Questions 21-23.

DIRECTIONS: Questions 21 through 23 are to be answered SOLELY on the basis of the following passage.

The need for the best in management techniques has given rise to the expression *scientific management*. Within reasonable limits, management can be scientific, but it will probably be many decades before it becomes truly scientific either in the factory or in the office. As long as it is impossible to measure accurately individual performance and to equate human behavior, so long will it be impossible to develop completely scientific techniques of office management. There is a likelihood, of course, that management might be reduced to a science when it is applied to inanimate objects which facilitate operations such as machinery, office equipment and furnishings, and forms. The limiting factor, therefore, is the human element.

21. The above passage is concerned PRIMARILY with the

    A. value of scientific office management
    B. methods for the development of scientific office management
    C. need for the best office management techniques
    D. possibility of reducing office management to a science

22. According to the above passage, the realization of truly scientific office management is dependent upon the

    A. expression of management techniques
    B. development of accurate personnel measurement techniques

C. passage of many decades, most probably
D. elimination of individual differences in human behavior

23. According to the above passage, the scientific management of inanimate objects 23.____

    A. occurs automatically because there is no human factor
    B. cannot occur in a factory, but can occur in an office
    C. could be achieved without the concurrent achievement of truly scientific office management
    D. is not a necessary component of truly scientific office management

Questions 24-25.

DIRECTIONS: Questions 24 and 25 are to be answered SOLELY on the basis of the following paragraph.

Your role as human resources utilization experts is to submit your techniques to operating administrators, for the program must, in reality, be theirs, not yours. We, in personnel, have been guilty of encouraging operating executives to believe that these important matters affecting their employees are personnel department matters, not management matters. We should hardly be surprised, as a consequence, to find these executives playing down the role of personnel and finding personnel routines a nuisance, for these are not in the mainstream of managing the enterprise – or so we have encouraged them to believe.

24. The BEST of the following interpretations of the above paragraph is that 24.____

    A. personnel people have been guilty of *passing the buck* on personnel functions
    B. operating officials have difficulty understanding personnel techniques
    C. personnel employees have tended to usurp some functions rightfully belonging to management
    D. matters affecting employees should be handled by the personnel department

25. The BEST of the following interpretations of the above paragraph is that 25.____

    A. personnel departments have aided and abetted the formulation of negative attitudes on the part of management
    B. personnel people are labor relations experts and should carry out these duties
    C. personnel activities are not really the responsibility of management
    D. management is now being encouraged by personnel experts to assume some responsibility for personnel functions

KEY (CORRECT ANSWERS)

1.	C	11.	B
2.	D	12.	C
3.	A	13.	D
4.	D	14.	B
5.	B	15.	C
6.	A	16.	B
7.	A	17.	C
8.	B	18.	D
9.	D	19.	B
10.	D	20.	D

21. D
22. B
23. C
24. C
25. A

TEST 3

DIRECTIONS: Each question or incomplete statement is followed by several suggested answers or completions. Select the one that BEST answers the question or completes the statement. *PRINT THE LETTER OF THE CORRECT ANSWER IN THE SPACE AT THE RIGHT.*

Questions 1-3

DIRECTIONS: Questions 1 through 3 are to be answered SOLELY on the basis of the following paragraph.

Prior to revising its child care program, a department feels that it is necessary to get some information from the mothers served by the existing program in order to determine where changes are required. A questionnaire is to be constructed to obtain this information.

1. Of the following points which can be taken into consideration in the construction of the questionnaire, the one which is of LEAST importance is

    A. that the data are to be put into punch cards
    B. the aspects of the program which seem to be in need of change
    C. the type of person who will fill out the questionnaire
    D. testing the questionnaire for ambiguity in advance of general distribution
    E. setting up a control group so that answers received can be compared to a standard

2. To discuss this questionnaire with all mothers who have been asked to answer it, before they actually fill it out, is

    A. *desirable;* the mothers may be able to offer valuable suggestions for changes in the form of the questionnaire
    B. *undesirable;* it is of some value but consumes too much valuable time
    C. *desirable;* cooperation and uniform interpretation will tend to be achieved
    D. *undesirable;* it may cause the answers to be biased
    E. *desirable;* the group will tend to support the program

3. Of the following items included in the questionnaire, the one which will be of LEAST assistance for comparing attitudes toward the program among different kinds of persons is

    A. name   B. address   C. age
    D. place of birth   E. education

Questions 4-6.

DIRECTIONS: Questions 4 through 6 are to be answered SOLELY on the basis of the following paragraph.

The supervisor of a large clerical and statistical division has assigned to one of the units under his supervision the preparation of a special statistical report required by the department head. The unit head accepted the assignment without comment but soon ran into considerable difficulty because no one in his unit had had any statistical training.

4. If a result of this lack of training is that the report is not completed on time, although everyone has done all that could be expected, the responsibility for the failure rests with

    A. the department head   B. the supervisor
    C. the unit head   D. the employees in the unit
    E. no one

5. This incident indicates that the supervisory staff has insufficient knowledge of employee

   A. capabilities
   B. reaction to increased demands
   C. on-the-job training needs
   D. work habits
   E. ability to perform ordinary assignments

6. After working on the report for two days, the unit head notifies the supervisor that he will not be able to get the report out in the required time. He states that his staff will be completely trained in another day or two and that after that preparing the report will be a simple matter. At this stage, the supervisor decides to have the statistical unit prepare the report. This action on the part of the supervisor is

   A. *undesirable;* the unit head should be given an incentive to continue with his training program which may produce good results
   B. *desirable;* it is the most effective way in which the supervisor can show his displeasure with the unit head's failure
   C. *undesirable;* it may adversely affect the morale of the unit
   D. *desirable;* it will generally result in a better report completed in a shorter time
   E. *undesirable;* the time spent on training the unit will be completely wasted

Questions 7-9.

DIRECTIONS: Questions 7 through 9 are to be answered SOLELY on the basis of the following paragraph.

The regressive uses of discipline are ubiquitous. Administrative architects who seek the optimum balance between structure and morale must accordingly look toward the identification and isolation of disciplinary elements. The whole range of disciplinary sanctions, from the reprimand to the dismissal, presents opportunities for reciprocity and accommodation of institutional interests. When rightly seized upon, these opportunities may provide the moment and the means for fruitful exercise of leadership and collaboration.

7. The one of the following ways of reworking the ideas presented in the above paragraph in order to be BEST suited for presentation in an in-service training course in supervision is:

   A. When one of your men does something wrong, talk it over with him. Tell him what he should have done. This is a chance for you to show the man that you are on his side and that you would welcome him on your side.
   B. It is not necessary to reprimand or to dismiss an employee because he needs disciplining. The alert foreman will lead and collaborate with his subordinates, making discipline unnecessary.
   C. A good way to lead the men you supervise is to take those opportunities which present themselves to use the whole range of disciplinary sanctions from reprimand to dismissal as a means for enforcing collaboration.
   D. Chances to punish a man in your squad should be welcomed as opportunities to show that you are a *good guy* who does not bear a grudge.
   E. Before you talk to a man or have him report to the office for something he has done wrong, attempt to lead him and get him to work with you. Tell him that his actions were wrong, that you expect him not to repeat the same wrong act, and that you will take a firmer stand if the act is repeated.

8. Of the following, the PRINCIPAL point made in the paragraph above is that

   A. discipline is frequently used improperly
   B. it is possible to isolate the factors entering into a disciplinary situation
   C. identification of the disciplinary elements is desirable
   D. disciplinary situations may be used to the advantage of the organization
   E. obtaining the best relationship between organizational form and spirit depends upon the ability to label disciplinary elements

9. The MOST novel idea presented in the above paragraph is that

   A. discipline is rarely necessary
   B. discipline may be a joint action of man and supervisor
   C. there are disciplinary elements which may be identified
   D. a range of disciplinary sanctions exists
   E. it is desirable to seek for balance between structure and morale.

Questions 10-11.

DIRECTIONS: Questions 10 and 11 are to be answered SOLELY on the basis of the following paragraph.

People must be selected to do the tasks involved and must be placed on a payroll in jobs fairly priced. Each of these people must be assigned those tasks which he can perform best; the work of each must be appraised, and good and poor work singled out appropriately. Skill in performing assigned tasks must be developed, and the total work situation must be conducive to sustained high performance. Finally, employees must be separated from the work force either voluntarily or involuntarily because of inefficient or unsatisfactory performance or because of curtailment of organizational activities.

10. A personnel function which is NOT included in the above description is

    A. classification   B. training   C. placement
    D. severance   E. service rating

11. The underlying implied purpose of the policy enunciated in the above paragraph is

    A. to plan for the curtailment of the organizational program when it becomes necessary
    B. to single out appropriate skill in performing assigned tasks
    C. to develop and maintain a high level of performance by employees
    D. that training employees in relation to the total work situation is essential if good and poor work are to be singled out
    E. that equal money for equal work results in a total work situation which insures proper appraisal

Questions 12-16.

DIRECTIONS: Questions 12 through 16 are to be answered SOLELY on the basis of the following sections which appeared in a report on the work production of two bureaus of a department. Throughout the report, assume that each month has 4 weeks.

Each of the two bureaus maintains a chronological file. In Bureau A, every 9 months on the average, this material fills a standard legal size file cabinet sufficient for 12,000 work units. In Bureau B, the same type of cabinet is filled in 18 months. Each bureau maintains three complete years of information plus a current file. When the current file cabinet is filled, the cabinet containing the oldest material is emptied, the contents disposed of, and the cabinet used for current material. The similarity of these operations makes it possible to consolidate these files with little effort.

Study of the practice of using typists as filing clerks for periods when there is no typing work showed (1) Bureau A has for the past 6 months completed a total of 1500 filing work units a week using on the average 200 man-hours of trained file clerk time and 20 man-hours of typist time, (2) Bureau B has in the same period completed a total of 2000 filing work units a week using on the average 125 man-hours of trained file clerk time and 60 hours of typist time. This includes all work in chronological files. Assuming that all clerks work at the same speed and that all typists work at the same speed, this indicates that work other than filing should be found for typists or that they should be given some training in the filing procedures used.... It should be noted that Bureau A has not been producing the 1,600 units of technical (not filing) work per 30 day period required by Schedule K, but is at present 200 units behind. The Bureau should be allowed 3 working days to get on schedule.

12. What percentage (approximate) of the total number of filing work units completed in both units consists of the work involved in the maintenance of the chronological files?

    A. 5% B. 10% C. 15% D. 20% E. 25%

13. If the two chronological files are consolidated, the number of months which should be allowed for filling a cabinet is

    A. 2 B. 4 C. 6 D. 8 E. 14

14. The MAXIMUM number of file cabinets which can be released for other uses as a result of the consolidation recommended is

    A. 0
    B. 1
    C. 2
    D. 3
    E. not determinable on the basis of the data given

15. If all the filing work for both units is consolidated without any diminution in the amount to be done and all filing work is done by trained file clerks, the number of clerks required (35-hour work week) is

    A. 4 B. 5 C. 6 D. 7 E. 8

16. In order to comply with the recommendation with respect to Schedule K, the present work production of Bureau A must be increased by

    A. 50%   B. 100%
    C. 150%   D. 200%
    E. an amount which is not determinable on the basis of the data given

Questions 17-18.

DIRECTIONS: Questions 17 and 18 are to be answered SOLELY on the basis of the following paragraph.

Production planning is mainly a process of synthesis. As a basis for the positive act of bringing complex production elements properly together, however, analysis is necessary, especially if improvement is to be made in an existing organization. The necessary analysis requires customary means of orientation and preliminary fact gathering with emphasis, however, on the recognition of administrative goals and of the relationship among work steps.

17. The entire process described is PRIMARILY one of

    A. taking apart, examining, and recombining
    B. deciding what changes are necessary, making the changes and checking on their value
    C. fact finding so as to provide the necessary orientation
    D. discovering just where the emphasis in production should be placed and then modifying the existing procedure so that it is placed properly
    E. recognizing administrative goals and the relationship among work steps

17.____

18. In production planning, according to the above paragraph, analysis is used PRIMARILY as

    A. a means of making important changes in an organization
    B. the customary means of orientation and preliminary fact finding
    C. a development of the relationship among work steps
    D. a means for holding the entire process intact by providing a logical basis
    E. a method to obtain the facts upon which a theory can be built

18.____

Questions 19-21.

DIRECTIONS: Questions 19 through 21 are to be answered SOLELY on the basis of the following paragraph.

Public administration is policy-making. But it is not autonomous, exclusive, or isolated policy-making. It is policy-making on a field where mighty forces contend, forces engendered in and by society. It is policy-making subject to still other and various policy makers. Public administration is one of a number of basic political processes by which these people achieve and control government.

19. From the point of view expressed in the above paragraph, public administration is

    A. becoming a technical field with completely objective processes
    B. the primary force in modern society
    C. a technical field which should be divorced from the actual decision-making function
    D. basically anti-democratic
    E. intimately related to politics

19.____

20. According to the above paragraph, public administration is NOT entirely   20.____

    A. a force generated in and by society
    B. subject at times to controlling influences
    C. a social process
    D. policy-making relating to administrative practices
    E. related to policy-making at lower levels

21. The above paragraph asserts that public administration   21.____

    A. develops the basic and controlling policies
    B. is the result of policies made by many different forces
    C. should attempt to break through its isolated policymaking and engage on a broader field
    D. is a means of directing government
    E. is subject to the political processes by which acts are controlled

Questions 22-24.

DIRECTIONS: Questions 22 through 24 are to be answered SOLELY on the basis of the following paragraph.

In order to understand completely the source of an employee's insecurity on his job, it is necessary to understand how he came to be, who he is, and what kind of a person he is away from his job. This would necessitate an understanding of those personal assets and liabilities which the employee brings to the job situation. These arise from his individual characteristics and his past experiences and established patterns of interpersonal relations. This whole area is of tremendous scope, encompassing everything included within the study of psychiatry and interpersonal relations. Therefore, it has been impracticable to consider it in detail. Attention has been focused on the relatively circumscribed area of the actual occupational situation. The factors considered – those which the employee brings to the job situation and which arise from his individual characteristics and his past experience and established patterns of interpersonal relations – are: intellectual level or capacity, specific aptitudes, education, work experience, health, social and economic background, patterns of interpersonal relations and resultant personality characteristics.

22. According to the above paragraph, the one of the following fields of study which would be of LEAST importance in the study of the problem is the   22.____

    A. relationships existing among employees
    B. causes of employee insecurity in the job situation
    C. conflict, if it exists, between intellectual level and work experience
    D. distribution of intellectual achievement
    E. relationship between employee characteristics and the established pattern of interpersonal relations in the work situation

23. According to the above paragraph, in order to make a thoroughgoing and comprehensive study of the sources of employee insecurity, the field of study should include   23.____

    A. only such circumscribed areas as are involved in extra-occupational situations
    B. a study of the dominant mores of the period
    C. all branches of the science of psychology

D. a determination of the characteristics, such as intellectual capacity, which an employee should bring to the job situation
E. employee personality characteristics arising from previous relationships with other people

24. It is implied by the above paragraph that it would be of GREATEST advantage to bring to this problem a comprehensive knowledge of

    A. all established patterns of interpersonal relations
    B. the milieu in which the employee group is located
    C. what assets and liabilities are presented in the job situation
    D. methods of focusing attention on relatively circumscribed regions
    E. the sources of an employee's insecurity on his job

24.____

Questions 25-26.

DIRECTIONS: Questions 25 and 26 are to be answered SOLELY on the basis of the following paragraph.

If, during a study, some hundreds of values of a variable (such as annual number of latenesses for each employee in a department) have been noted merely in the arbitrary order in which they happen to occur, the mind cannot properly grasp the significance of the record; the observations must be ranked or classified in some way before the characteristics of the series can be comprehended, and those comparisons, on which arguments as to causation depend, can be made with other series. A dichotomous classification is too crude; if the values are merely classified according to whether they exceed or fall short of some fixed value, a large part of the information given by the original record is lost. Numerical measurements lend themselves with peculiar readiness to a manifold classification.

25. According to the above paragraph, if the values of a variable which are gathered during a study are classified in a few subdivisions, the MOST likely result will be

    A. an inability to grasp the significance of the record
    B. an inability to relate the series with other series
    C. a loss of much of the information in the original data
    D. a loss of the readiness with which numerical measurements lend themselves to a manifold classification
    E. that the order in which they happen to occur will be arbitrary

25.____

26. The above paragraph advocates, with respect to numerical data, the use of

    A. arbitrary order
    B. comparisons with other series
    C. a two value classification
    D. a many value classification
    E. all values of a variable

26.____

Question 27.

DIRECTIONS: Question 27 is to be answered SOLELY on the basis of the following paragraph.

A more significant manifestation of the concern of the community with the general welfare is the collection and dissemination of statistics. This statement may cause the reader to smile, for statistics seem to be drab and prosaic things. The great growth of statistics, however, is one of the most remarkable characteristics of the age. Never before has a community kept track from month to month, and in some cases from week to week, of how many people are born, how many die and from what causes, how many are sick, how much is being produced, how much is being sold, how many people are at work, how many people are unemployed, how long they have been out of work, what prices people pay, how much income they receive and from what sources, how much they owe, what they intend to buy. These elaborate attempts of the country to keep informed about what is happening mean that the community is concerned with how its members are faring and with the conditions under which they live. For this reason, the present age may take pride in its numerous and regular statistical reports and in the rapid increase in the number of these reports. No other age has evidenced such a keen interest in the conditions of the people.

27. The writer implies that statistics are   27.____

    A. too scientific for general use
    B. too elaborate and too drab
    C. related to the improvement of living conditions
    D. frequently misinterpreted
    E. a product of the machine age

KEY (CORRECT ANSWERS)

1. E   11. C
2. C   12. C
3. A   13. C
4. B   14. B
5. A   15. D

6. D   16. E
7. A   17. A
8. D   18. E
9. B   19. E
10. A   20. D

21. D
22. D
23. E
24. B
25. C
26. D
27. C

INTERPRETING STATISTICAL DATA GRAPHS, CHARTS AND TABLES

EXAMINATION SECTION

TEST 1

DIRECTIONS: Each question or incomplete statement is followed by several suggested answers or completions. Select the one that BEST answers the question or completes the statement. *PRINT THE LETTER OF THE CORRECT ANSWER IN THE SPACE AT THE RIGHT.*

Questions 1-10.

DIRECTIONS: Questions 1 through 10 are to be answered SOLELY on the basis of the following table showing the amounts purchased by various purchasing units during 2020.

DOLLAR VOLUME PURCHASED BY EACH PURCHASING UNIT DURING EACH QUARTER OF 2020 (FIGURES SHOWN REPRESENT THOUSANDS OF DOLLARS)				
Purchasing Unit	First Quarter	Second Quarter	Third Quarter	Fourth Quarter
A	578	924	698	312
B	1,426	1,972	1,586	1,704
C	366	494	430	716
D	1,238	1,708	1,884	1,546
E	730	742	818	774
F	948	1,118	1,256	788

1. The total dollar volume purchased by all of the purchasing units during 2020 approximated MOST NEARLY
   A. $2,000,000   B. $4,000,000   C. $20,000,000   D. $40,000,000

    1.____

2. During which quarter was the GREATEST total dollar amount of purchases made?
   A. First   B. Second   C. Third   D. Fourth

    2.____

3. Assume that the dollar volume purchased by Unit F during 2020 exceeded the dollar volume purchased by Unit F during 2019 by 50%.
   Then, the dollar volume purchased by Unit F during 2019 was
   A. $2,055,000   B. $2,550,000   C. $2,740,000   D. $6,165,000

    3.____

4. Which one of the following purchasing units showed the sharpest DECREASE in the amount purchased during the fourth quarter as compared with the third quarter?
   A. A   B. B   C. D   D. E

    4.____

121

2 (#1)

5. Comparing the dollar volume purchased in the second quarter with the dollar volume purchased in the third quarter, the decrease in the dollar volume during the third quarter was PRIMARILY due to the decrease in the dollar volume purchased by Units

   A. A and B   B. C and D   C. C and E   D. C and F

5.____

6. Of the following, the unit which had the LARGEST number of dollars of increased purchases from any one quarter to the next following quarter was Unit

   A. A   B. B   C. C   D. D

6.____

7. Of the following, the unit with the LARGEST dollar volume of purchases during the second half of 2020 was Unit

   A. A   B. B   C. D   D. F

7.____

8. Which one of the following MOST closely approximates the percentage which Unit B's total 2020 purchases represents the total 2020 purchases of all units, including Unit B?

   A. 10%   B. 15%   C. 25%   D. 45%

8.____

9. Assume that research showed that each ten thousand dollars ($10,000) of purchases by Unit D during 2020 required an average of thirteen (13) man-hours of buyers' staff time.
   On that basis, which one of the following MOST closely approximates the number of man-hours of buyers' staff time required by Unit D during 2020?
   _____ man-hours.

   A. 1,800   B. 8,000   C. 68,000   D. 78,000

9.____

10. Assume that research showed that each ten thousand dollars ($10,000) of purchases by Unit C during 020 required an average of ten (10) man-hours of buyers' staff time. This research also showed that during 2020 the average man-hours of buyers' staff time per ten thousand dollars of purchases required by Unit C exceeded by 25% the average man-hours of buyers' staff time per ten thousand dollars of purchases required by Unit E.
    On that basis, which one of the following MOST closely approximates the number of buyers' staff man-hours required by Unit E during 2020?
    _____ man-hours.

    A. 2,200   B. 2,400   C. 3,000   D. 3,700

10.____

KEY (CORRECT ANSWERS)

1. C
2. B
3. C
4. A
5. A
6. B
7. C
8. C
9. B
10. B

TEST 2

Questions 1-6.

DIRECTIONS: Questions 1 through 6 are to be answers SOLELY on the basis of the information contained in the five charts below. *PRINT THE LETTER OF THE CORRECT ANSWER IN THE SPACE AT THE RIGHT.*

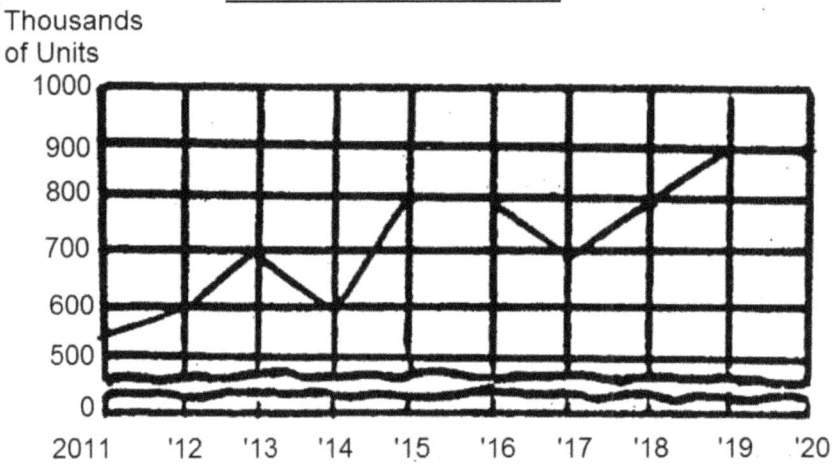

NUMBER OF UNITS OF WORK PRODUCED IN THE BUREAU PER YEAR

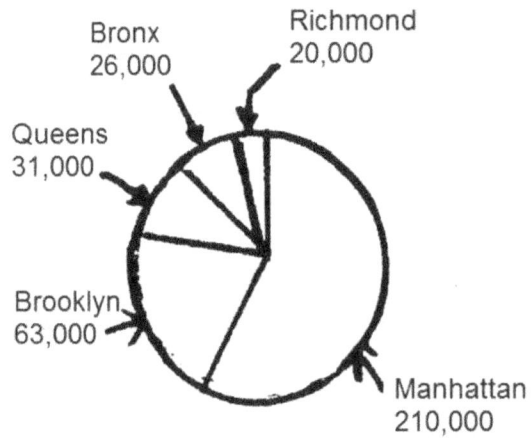

INCREASE IN THE NUMBER OF UNITS OF WORK PRODUCED IN 2020 OVER THE NUMBER PRODUCED IN 2011, BY BOROUGH

Bronx 26,000
Richmond 20,000
Queens 31,000
Brooklyn 63,000
Manhattan 210,000

NUMBER OF MALE AND FEMALE EMPLOYEES PRODUCING THE UNITS OF WORK IN THE BUREAU PER YEAR

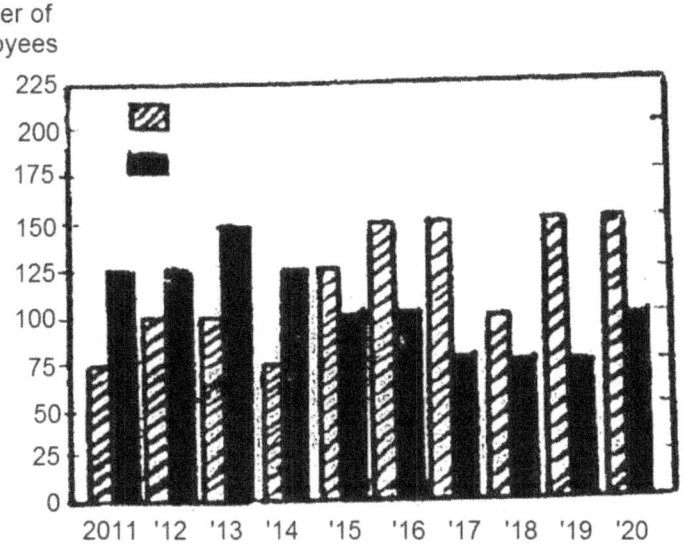

DISTRIBUTION OF THE AGES BY PERCENT OF EMPLOYEES ASSIGNED TO PRODUCE THE UNITS OF WORK IN THE YEARS 2011 AND 2020

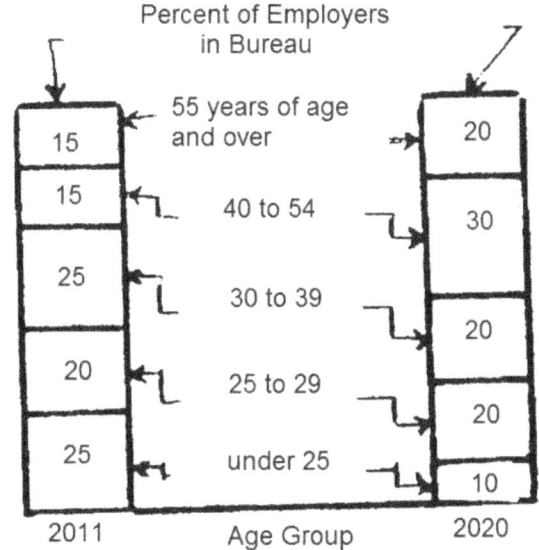

3 (#2)

TOTAL SALARIES PAID PER YEAR TO EMPLOYEES ASSIGNED TO PRODUCE THE UNITS OF WORK IN THE BUREAU

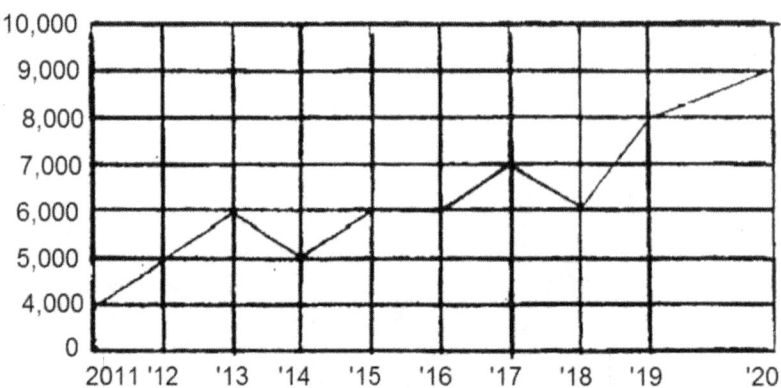

1. The information contained in the charts is sufficient to determine the
    A. amount of money paid in salaries to employees working in Richmond in 2020
    B. difference between the average annual salary of employees in the Bureau in 2020 and their average annual salary in 2019
    C. number of female employees in the Bureau between 30 and 39 years of age who were employed in 2011
    D. cost, in salary, for the average male employee in the Bureau to produce 100 units of work in 2016

1.____

2. The one of the following which was GREATER in the Bureau in 2016 than it was in 2014 was the
    A. cost, in salaries, of producing a unit of work
    B. units of work produced annually per employee
    C. proportion of female employees to total number of employees
    D. average annual salary per employee

2.____

3. If, in 2020, one-half of the employees in the Bureau 55 years of age and over each earned an annual salary of $42,000, then the average annual salary of all the remaining employees in the Bureau was MOST NEARLY
    A. $31,750   B. $34,500   C. $35,300   D. $35,800

3.____

4. Assume that, in 2011, the offices in Richmond and the Bronx each produced the same number of units of work. Also assume that, in 2011, the offices in Brooklyn, Manhattan, and Queens each produced twice as many units of work as were produced in either of the other two boroughs.
    Then, the number of units of work produced in Brooklyn in 2010 was MOST NEARLY
    A. 69,000   B. 138,000   C. 201,000   D. 225,000

4.____

5. If, in 2008, the average annual salary of the female employees in the Bureau was four-fifths as large as the average annual salary of the male employees, then the average annual salary of the female employees in that year was
   A. $37,500   B. $31,000   C. $30,500   D. $30,000

   5._____

6. Of the total number of employees in the Bureau who were 30 years of age and over in 2011, _____ must have been _____.
   A. at least 35; females
   B. less than 75; males
   C. no more than 100; females
   D. more than 15; males

   6._____

KEY (CORRECT ANSWERS)

1.	B	4.	C
2.	B	5.	D
3.	C	6.	A

TEST 3

Questions 1-10.

DIRECTIONS: Questions 1 through 10 are to be answered SOLELY on the basis of the REPORT OF TELEPHONE CALLS table given below. *PRINT THE LETTER OF THE CORRECT ANSWER IN THE SPACE AT THE RIGHT.*

	TABLE – REPORT OF TELEPHONE CALLS						
Dept.	No. of Stations	No. of Employees	No. of Incoming Calls		No. of Long Distance Calls		No. of Divisions
			2019	2020	2019	2020	
I	11	40	3421	4292	72	54	5
II	36	220	10392	10191	75	78	18
III	53	250	85243	85084	103	98	8
IV	24	60	9675	10123	82	85	6
V	13	30	5208	5492	54	48	6
VI	25	35	7472	8109	86	90	5
VII	37	195	11412	11299	68	72	11
VIII	36	54	8467	8674	59	68	4
IX	163	306	294321	289968	289	321	13
X	40	83	9588	8266	93	89	5
XI	24	68	7867	7433	86	87	13
XII	50	248	10039	10208	101	95	30
XIII	10	230	7550	6941	28	21	10
XIV	25	103	14281	14392	48	40	5
XV	19	230	8475	9206	38	43	8
XVI	22	45	4684	5584	39	48	10
XVII	41	58	10102	9677	49	52	6
XVIII	82	106	106242	105899	128	132	10
XIX	6	13	2649	2498	35	29	2
XX	16	30	1395	1468	7890	2	

1. The department which had more than 106,000 incoming calls in 2019 but fewer than 250,000 is 1.____
   A. II   B. IX   C. XVIII   D. III

2. The department which has fewer than 8 divisions and more than 100 but fewer than 300 employees is 2.____
   A. VII   B. XIV   C. XV   D. XVIII

3. The department which had an increase in 2020 over 2019 in the number of both incoming and long distance calls but had an increase in long distance calls of not more than 3 is 3.____
   A. IV   B. VI   C. XVII   D. XVIII

128

4. The department which had a decrease in the number of incoming calls in 2020 as compared to 2019 and has not less than 6 nor more than 7 divisions is
 A. IV B. V C. XVII D. III

4._____

5. The department which has more than 7 divisions and more than 200 employees but fewer than 19 stations is
 A. XV B. III C. XX D. XIII

5._____

6. The department having more than 10 divisions and fewer than 36 stations, which had an increase in long distance calls in 2020 over 2019 is
 A. XI B. VII C. XVI D. XVIII

6._____

7. The department which in 2020 had at least 7,250 incoming calls and a decrease in long distance calls from 2019, and has more than 50 stations is
 A. IX B. XII C. XVIII D. III

7._____

8. The department which has fewer than 25 stations, fewer than 100 employees, 10 or more divisions, and showed an increase of at least 9 long distance calls in 2020 over 2019 is
 A. IX B. XVI C. XX D. XIII

8._____

9. The department which has more than 50 but fewer than 125 employee and had more than 5,000 incoming calls in 2019 but not more than 10,000, and more than 60 long distance calls in 2020 but not more than 85, and has more than 24 stations is
 A. VIII B. XIV C. IV D. XI

9._____

10. If the number of departments showing an increase in long distance calls in 2020 over 2019 exceeds the number showing a decrease in long distance calls in the same period, select the Roman numeral indicating the department having less than one station for each 10 employees, provided not more than 8 divisions are served by that department.
 If the number of departments showing an increase in long distance calls in 2020 over 2019 does not exceed the number showing a decrease in long distance calls in the same period, select the Roman numeral indicating the department having the SMALLEST number of incoming calls in 2020.
 A. III B. XIII C. XV D. XX

10._____

KEY (CORRECT ANSWERS)

1. C
2. B
3. A
4. C
5. D
6. A
7. D
8. B
9. A
10. C

TEST 4

Questions 1-7.

DIRECTIONS: Questions 1 through 7 are to be answered SOLELY on the basis of the following chart. *PRINT THE LETTER OF THE CORRECT ANSWER IN THE SPACE AT THE RIGHT.*

EMPLOYABILITY CLASSIFICATION OF PERSONS RECEIVING HOME RELIEF OR VETERANS' ASSISTANCE AT WELFARE CENTER V, JANUARY 1, THIS YEAR				
Employability	Home Relief		Veterans' Assistance	
Classification	Full	Supplementary	Full	Supplementary
Employable	369	207	15	42
Employed	330	83	2	35
Not Available for Employment	550	129	27	93
Awaiting employment conference	24	4	1	3
In rehabilitation	81	18	1	21
Attending school	26	16	3	13
In training	78	24	4	4
Temporary family care duties	32	19	6	7
Permanent family care duties	166	7	8	25
Unverified health condition	77	22	1	3
Temporary health condition	66	19	3	17
Permanently unemployable	47	8	1	37
TOTAL	1296	427	45	207

1. Of the persons on Home Relief who are either employed or employable, the percentage who are employable and are receiving full assistance is MOST NEARLY
   A. 30%   B. 35%   C. 50%   D. 65%

   1.____

2. Assume that it is possible each month to reduce the number of Home Relief clients who are not available for employment and who are receiving full assistance by 10% from the previous month.
   By June 1, this year, the number of such Home Relief clients would be MOST NEARLY
   A. 225   B. 275   C. 325   D. 375

   2.____

3. During the month of January, this year, of the full-assistance clients on Home Relief who were not available for employment because of temporary health conditions, 42% were removed from the relief rolls, and another 26% were reassigned to supplementary Home Relief assistance because of temporary health conditions.
   Taking figures to the nearest whole number, the number of all remaining Home Relief clients, including both full and supplementary assistance at Welfare Center V is MOST NEARLY
   A. 1250   B. 1265   C. 1675   D. 1695

   3.____

4. The one of the following figures which is MOST likely to require checking for accuracy or investigating for significance is the figure for persons
   A. not available for employment who are receiving supplementary Veterans' Assistance
   B. receiving full Home Relief assistance who are employed
   C. receiving supplementary Home Relief assistance who are not available for employment because they are in rehabilitation
   D. receiving supplementary Veterans' Assistance who are permanently unemployable

5. With regard to clients receiving full Veterans' Assistance, the average monthly allotment per client in the various categories is as follows: Employable $168.06; Employed $194.92; Not Available for Employment $130.74; and Permanently Unemployable $112.56.
   The average monthly allotment for all clients receiving full Veterans' Assistance at Welfare Center V is MOST NEARLY
   A. $140.06   B. $145.64   C. $151.58   D. $162.26

6. If all the Employable Home Relief clients on full assistance were to find employment so that 2/3 of them would no longer need any assistance and the rest would need only supplementary assistance, then the ratio of all Home Relief clients on full assistance to all Home Relief clients on supplementary assistance would be MOST NEARLY
   A. 2:1   B. 3:1   C. 3:2   D. 5:3

7. Assume that, for the category of Veterans' Assistance, the Federal government were to pay 2/3 of the first $60 of assistance given to each client, and 1/2 of the balance, on the basis of the average amount of assistance given to all veterans at a welfare center. Assume further that the average supplementary assistance given is $72, and the average full assistance is $140 at Welfare Center V.
   Under this plan, the amount of Veterans' Assistance given by Welfare Center V for which they would be reimbursed by the Federal government will be MOST NEARLY
   A. $8,000   B. $11,000   C. $13,000   D. $17,000

KEY (CORRECT ANSWERS)

1. B   5. B
2. C   6. D
3. D   7. C
4. B

TEST 5

Questions 1-10.

DIRECTIONS: Questions 1 through 10 are to be answered SOLELY on the basis of the Personnel Record of Division X shown below. *PRINT THE LETTER OF THE CORRECT ANSWER IN THE SPACE AT THE RIGHT.*

		DIVISION X PERSONNEL RECORD – CURRENT YEAR				
Employee	Bureau in Which Employed	Title	Annual Salary	No. of Days Absent		No. of Times Late
				On Vacation	On Sick Leave	
Abbott	Mail	Clerk	$31,200	18	0	1
Barnes	Mail	Clerk	$25,200	25	3	7
Davis	Mail	Typist	$24,000	21	9	2
Adams	Payroll	Accountant	$42,500	10	0	2
Bell	Payroll	Bookkeeper	$31,200	23	2	5
Duke	Payroll	Clerk	$27,600	24	4	3
Gross	Payroll	Clerk	$21,600	12	5	7
Lane	Payroll	Stenographer	$26,400	19	16	20
Reed	Payroll	Typist	$22,800	15	11	11
Arnold	Record	Clerk	$32,400	6	15	9
Cane	Record	Clerk	$24,500	14	3	4
Fay	Record	Clerk	$21,100	20	0	4
Hale	Record	Typist	$25,200	18	2	7
Baker	Supply	Clerk	$30,000	20	3	2
Clark	Supply	Clerk	$27,600	25	6	5
Ford	Supply	Typist	$22,800	25	4	22

1. The percentage of the total number of employees who are clerks is MOST NEARLY
   A. 25%   B. 33%   C. 38%   D. 56%

2. Of the following employees, the one who receives a monthly salary of $2,100 is
   A. Barnes   B. Gross   C. Reed   D. Clark

3. The difference between the annual salary of the highest paid clerk and that of the lowest paid clerk is
   A. $6,000   B. $8,400   C. $11,300   D. $20,900

4. The number of employees receiving more than $25,000 a year but less than $40,000 a year is
   A. 6   B. 9   C. 12   D. 15

5. The TOTAL annual salary of the employees of the Mail Bureau is _____ the total annual salary of the employees of the _____.
   A. one-half of; Payroll Bureau
   B. less than; Record Bureau by $21,600
   C. equal to; Supply Bureau
   D. less than; Payroll Bureau by $71,600

2 (#5)

6. The average annual salary of the employees who are not clerks is MOST NEARLY
   A. $23,700   B. $25,450   C. $26,800   D. $27,850

7. If all the employees were given a 10% increase in pay, the annual salary of Lane would then be
   A. *greater* than that of Barnes by $1,320
   B. *less* than that of Bell by $4,280
   C. *equal* to that of Clark
   D. *greater* than that of Ford by $3,600

8. Of the clerks who earned less than $30,000 a year, the one who was late the FEWEST number of times was late _____ time(s).
   A. 1   B. 2   C. 3   D. 4

9. The bureau in which the employees were late the FEWEST number of times on an average age is the _____ Bureau.
   A. Mail   B. Payroll   C. Record   D. Supply

10. The MOST accurate of the following statements is that:
    A. Reed was late more often than any other typist
    B. Bell took more time off for vacation than any other employee earning $30,000 or more annually
    C. of the typist, Ford was the one who was absent the fewest number of times
    D. three clerks took no time off because of sickness

KEY (CORRECT ANSWERS)

1.	D	6.	D
2.	A	7.	A
3.	C	8.	C
4.	B	9.	A
5.	C	10.	B

TEST 6

Questions 1-8.

DIRECTIONS: Questions 1 through 8 are to be answered SOLELY on the basis of the information contained in the chart and table shown below which relate to Bureau X in a certain public agency. The chart shows the percentage of the bureau's annual expenditures spent on equipment, supplies, and salaries for each of the years 2016-2020. The table shows the bureau's annual expenditures for each of the years 2016-2020. *PRINT THE LETTER OF THE CORRECT ANSWER IN THE SPACE AT THE RIGHT.*

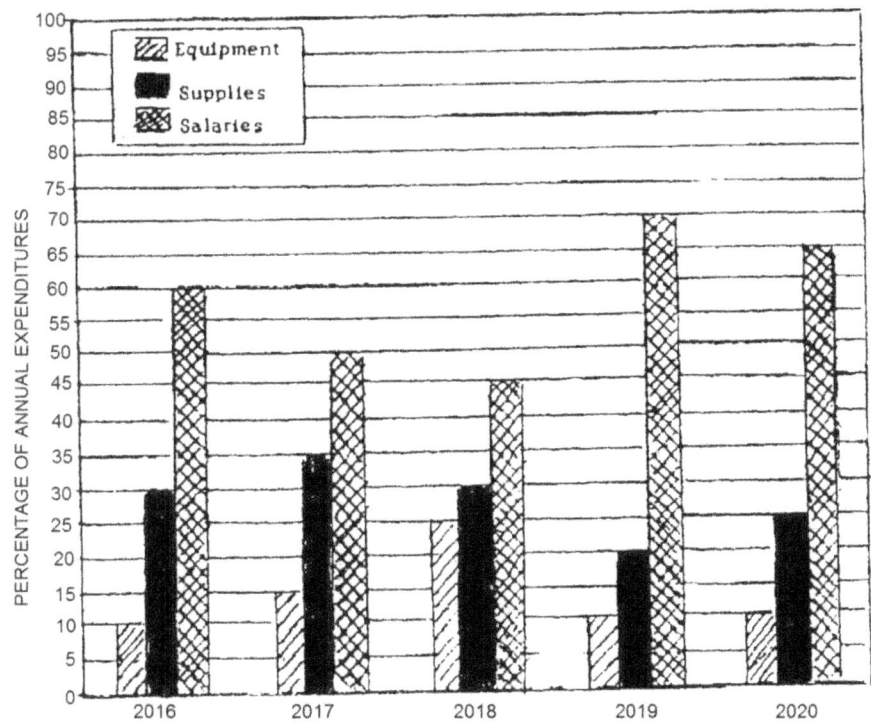

The bureau's annual expenditures for the years 2016-2020 are shown in the following table:

YEAR	EXPENDITURES
2016	$8,000,000
2017	$12,000,000
2018	$15,000,000
2019	$10,000,000
2020	$12,000,000

Equipment, supplies, and salaries were the only three categories for which the bureau spent money.

2 (#6)

Candidates may find it useful to arrange their computations on their scratch paper in an orderly manner since the correct computations for one question may also be helpful in answering another question.

1. The information contained in the chart and table is sufficient to determine the
   A. average annual salary of an employee in the bureau in 2017
   B. decrease in the amount of money spent on supplies in the bureau in 2016 from the amount spent in the preceding year
   C. changes between 2018 and 2019 in the prices of supplies bought by the bureau
   D. increase in the amount of money spent on salaries in the bureau in 2020 over the amount spent in the preceding year

2. If the percentage of expenditures for salaries in one year is added to the percentage of expenditures for equipment in that year, a total of two percentages for that year is obtained.
   The two years for which this total is the SAME are
   A. 2016 and 2018
   B. 2017 and 2019
   C. 2016 and 2019
   D. 2017 and 2020

3. Of the following, the year in which the bureau spent the GREATEST amount of money on supplies was
   A. 2020   B. 2018   C. 2017   D. 2016

4. Of the following years, the one in which there was the GREATEST increase over the preceding year in the amount of money spent on salaries is
   A. 2019   B. 2020   C. 2017   D. 2018

5. Of the bureau's expenditures for equipment in 2020, one-third was used for the purchase of mailroom equipment and the remainder was spent on miscellaneous office equipment.
   How much did the bureau spend on miscellaneous office equipment in 2020?
   A. $4,000,000   B. $400,000   C. $8,000,000   D. $800,000

6. If there were 120 employees in the bureau in 2019, then the average annual salary paid to the employees in that year was MOST NEARLY
   A. $43,450   B. $49,600   C. $58,350   D. $80,800

7. In 2018, the bureau had 125 employees.
   If 20 of the employees earned an average annual salary of $80,000, then the average salary of the other 105 employees was MOST NEARLY
   A. $49,000   B. $64,000   C. $41,000   D. $54,000

3 (#6)

8. Assume that the bureau estimated that the amount of money it would spend on supplies in 2021 would be the same as the amount it spent on that category in 2020. Similarly, the bureau estimated that the amount of money it would spend on equipment in 2021 would be the same as the amount it spent on that category in 2020. However, the bureau estimated that in 2021 the amount it would spent on salaries would be 10 percent higher than the amount it spent on that category in 2020.
The percentage of its annual expenditures that the bureau estimated it would spend on supplies in 2021 is MOST NEARLY
   A. 27.5%   B. 23.5%   C. 22.5%   D. 25%

8._____

KEY (CORRECT ANSWERS)

1.	D	5.	D
2.	A	5.	C
3.	B	7.	A
4.	C	8.	B

TEST 7

Questions 1-5.

DIRECTIONS: Column I lists five kinds of statistical data which are to be transformed into a chart or a graph for incorporation into the department annual report. Column II lists nine different kinds of graphs or charts. For each type of information listed in Column I, select the chart or graph from Column II by means of which it should be demonstrated. *PRINT THE LETTER OF THE CORRECT ANSWER IN THE SPACE AT THE RIGHT.*

Column I

1. The relationship between employees' occupational classification and their salaries, for all employees by occupational classification, showing minimum, maximum, and average salary in each group.

2. A comparison of the number of employees in the department, the departmental budget, the number of employees in the operating divisions and the operating division budget for each year over a ten-year period.

3. The amount of money spent for each of department's 10 most important functions during the past year

4. The percentage of the department's budget spent for each of the department's activities for each year over a ten-year period.

5. The number of each kind of employee employed in the department over a period of twenty years and the total number of employees in the department for each of these periods.

Column II

A.

B. (pie chart)

C. (bar chart)

D. (line graph)

E. (stacked area chart)

F. (scatter plot with + marks)

G.

H. (stacked bar chart)

1.____

2.____

3.____

4.____

5.____

KEY (CORRECT ANSWERS)

1. F
2. D
3. C
4. H
5. G

RECORD KEEPING
EXAMINATION SECTION
TEST 1

DIRECTIONS: Each question or incomplete statement is followed by several suggested answers or completions. Select the one that BEST answers the question or completes the statement. *PRINT THE LETTER OF THE CORRECT ANSWER IN THE SPACE AT THE RIGHT.*

Questions 1-7.

DIRECTIONS: In answering Questions 1 through 7, use the following master list. For each question, determine where the name would fit on the master list. Each answer choice indicates right before or after the name in the answer choice.

    Aaron, Jane
    Armstead, Brendan
    Bailey, Charles
    Dent, Ricardo
    Grant, Mark
    Mars, Justin
    Methieu, Justine
    Parker, Cathy
    Sampson, Suzy
    Thomas, Heather

1. Schmidt, William
   A. Right before Cathy Parker
   B. Right after Heather Thomas
   C. Right after Suzy Sampson
   D. Right before Ricardo Dent

1.____

2. Asanti, Kendall
   A. Right before Jane Aaron
   B. Right after Charles Bailey
   C. Right before Justine Methieu
   D. Right after Brendan Armstead

2.____

3. O'Brien, Daniel
   A. Right after Justine Methieu
   B. Right before Jane Aaron
   C. Right after Mark Grant
   D. Right before Suzy Sampson

3.____

4. Marrow, Alison
   A. Right before Cathy Parker
   B. Right before Justin Mars
   C. Right before Mark Grant
   D. Right after Heather Thomas

4.____

5. Grantt, Marissa
   A. Right before Mark Grant
   B. Right after Mark Grant
   C. Right after Justin Mars
   D. Right before Suzy Sampson

5.____

6. Thompson, Heath   6.____
   A. Right after Justin Mars   B. Right before Suzy Sampson
   C. Right after Heather Thomas D. Right before Cathy Parker

DIRECTIONS: Before answering Question 7, add in all of the names from Questions 1 through 6. Then fit the name in alphabetical order based on the new list.

7. Francisco, Mildred   7.____
   A. Right before Mark Grant   B. Right after Marissa Grantt
   C. Right before Alison Marrow D. Right after Kendall Asanti

Questions 8-10.

DIRECTIONS: In answering Questions 8 through 10, compare each pair of names and addresses. Indicate whether they are the same or different in any way.

8. William H. Pratt, J.D.   William H. Pratt, J.D.   8.____
   Attourney at Law   Attorney at Law
   A. No differences   B. 1 difference
   C. 2 differences   D. 3 differences

9. 1303 Theater Drive,; Apt. 3-B   1330 Theatre Drive,; Apt. 3-B   9.____
   A. No differences   B. 1 difference
   C. 2 differences   D. 3 differences

10. Petersdorff, Briana and Mary   Petersdorff, Briana and Mary   10.____
    A. No differences   B. 1 difference
    C. 2 differences   D. 3 differences

11. Which of the following words, if any, are misspelled?   11.____
    A. Affordable   B. Circumstansial
    C. Legalese   D. None of the above

Questions 12-13.

DIRECTIONS: Questions 12 and 13 are to be answered on the basis of the following table.

Standardized Test Results for High School Students in District #1230

	English	Math	Science	Reading
High School 1	21	22	15	18
High School 2	12	16	13	15
High School 3	16	18	21	17
High School 4	19	14	15	16

The scores for each high school in the district were averaged out and listed for each subject tested. Scores of 0-10 are significantly below College Readiness Standards. 11-15 are below College Readiness, 16-20 meet College Readiness, and 21-25 are above College Readiness.

12. If the high schools need to meet or exceed in at least half the categories in order to NOT be considered "at risk," which schools are considered "at risk"? 12.____
    A. High School 2   B. High School 3
    C. High School 4   D. Both A and C

13. What percentage of subjects did the district as a whole meet or exceed College Readiness standards? 13.____
    A. 25%   B. 50%   C. 75%   D. 100%

Questions 14-15.

DIRECTIONS: Questions 14 and 15 are to be answered on the basis of the following information.

You have seven employees working as a part of your team: Austin, Emily, Jeremy, Christina, Martin, Harriet, and Steve. You have just sent an e-mail informing them that there will be a mandatory training session next week. To ensure that work still gets done, you are offering the training twice during the week: once on Tuesday and also on Thursday. This way half the employees will still be working while the other half attend the training. The only other issue is that Jeremy doesn't work on Tuesdays and Harriet doesn't work on Thursdays due to compressed work schedules.

14. Which of the following is a possible attendance roster for the first training session? 14.____
    A. Emily, Jeremy, Steve   B. Steve, Christina, Harriet
    C. Harriet, Jeremy, Austin   D. Steve, Martin, Jeremy

15. If Harriet, Christina, and Steve attend the training session on Tuesday, which of the following is a possible roster for Thursday's training session? 15.____
    A. Jeremy, Emily, and Austin   B. Emily, Martin, and Harriet
    C. Austin, Christina, and Emily   D. Jeremy, Emily, and Steve

Questions 16-20.

DIRECTIONS: In answering Questions 16 through 20, you will be given a word and will need to choose the answer choice that is MOST similar or different to the word.

16. Which word means the SAME as *annual*? 16.____
    A. Monthly   B. Usually   C. Yearly   D. Constantly

17. Which word means the SAME as *effort*? 17.____
    A. Energy   B. Equate   C. Cherish   D. Commence

18. Which word means the OPPOSITE of *forlorn*? 18.____
    A. Neglected B. Lethargy   C. Optimistic D. Astonished

19. Which word means the SAME as *risk*? 19.____
    A. Admire   B. Hazard   C. Limit   D. Hesitant

20. Which word means the OPPOSITE of *translucent*?   20.____
    A. Opaque   B. Transparent   C. Luminous   D. Introverted

21. Last year, Jamie's annual salary was $50,000. Her boss called her today   21.____
    to inform her that she would receive a 20% raise for the upcoming year. How
    much more money will Jamie receive next year?
    A. $60,000   B. $10,000   C. $1,000   D. $51,000

22. You and a co-worker work for a temp hiring agency as part of their office   22.____
    staff. You both are given 6 days off per month. How many days off are you
    and your co-worker given in a year?
    A. 24   B. 72   C. 144   D. 48

23. If Margot makes $34,000 per year and she works 40 hours per week for   23.____
    all 52 weeks, what is her hourly rate?
    A. $16.34/hour   B. $17.00/hour   C. $15.54/hour   D. $13.23/hour

24. How many dimes are there in $175.00?   24.____
    A. 175   B. 1,750   C. 3,500   D. 17,500

25. If Janey is three times as old as Emily, and Emily is 3, how old is Janey?   25.____
    A. 6   B. 9   C. 12   D. 15

KEY (CORRECT ANSWERS)

1.	C		11.	B
2.	D		12.	A
3.	A		13.	D
4.	B		14.	B
5.	B		15.	A
6.	C		16.	C
7.	A		17.	A
8.	B		18.	C
9.	C		19.	B
10.	A		20.	A

21. B
22. C
23. A
24. B
25. B

TEST 2

DIRECTIONS: Each question or incomplete statement is followed by several suggested answers or completions. Select the one that BEST answers the question or completes the statement. *PRINT THE LETTER OF THE CORRECT ANSWER IN THE SPACE AT THE RIGHT.*

Questions 1-6.

DIRECTIONS: Questions 1 through 6 are to be answered on the basis of the following information.

item	name of item to be ordered
quantity	minimum number that can be ordered
beginning amount	amount in stock at start of month
amount received	amount receiving during month
ending amount	amount in stock at end of month
amount used	amount used during month
amount to order	will need at least as much of each item as used in the previous month
unit price	cost of each unit of an item
total price	total price for the order

Item	Quantity	Beginning	Received	Ending	Amount Used	Amount to Order	Unit Price	Total Price
Pens	10	22	10	8	24	20	$0.11	$2.20
Spiral notebooks	8	30	13	12			$0.25	
Binder clips	2 boxes	3 boxes	1 box	1 box			$1.79	
Sticky notes	3 packs	12 packs	4 packs	2 packs			$1.29	
Dry erase markers	1 pack (dozen)	34 markers	8 markers	40 markers			$16.49	
Ink cartridges (printer)	1 cartridge	3 cartridges	1 cartridge	2 cartridges			$79.99	
Folders	10 folders	25 folders	15 folders	10 folders			$1.08	

1. How many packs of sticky notes were used during the month? 1.____
   A. 16   B. 10   C. 12   D. 14

2. How many folders need to be ordered for next month? 2.____
   A. 15   B. 20   C. 30   D. 40

3. What is the total price of notebooks that you will need to order? 3.____
   A. $6.00   B. $0.25   C. $4.50   D. $2.75

4. Which of the following will you spend the second most money on? 4.____
   A. Ink cartridges   B. Dry erase markers
   C. Sticky notes   D. Binder clips

5. How many packs of dry erase markers should you order? 5.____
   A. 1   B. 8   C. 12   D. 0

6. What will be the total price of the file folders you order? 6.____
   A. $20.16   B. $21.60   C. $10.80   D. $4.32

Questions 7-11.

DIRECTIONS: Questions 7 through 11 are to be answered on the basis of the following table.

Number of Car Accidents, By Location and Cause, for 2014						
	Location 1		Location 2		Location 3	
Cause	Number	Percent	Number	Percent	Number	Percent
Severe Weather	10		25		30	
Excessive Speeding	20	40	5		10	
Impaired Driving	15		15	25	8	
Miscellaneous	5		15		2	4
TOTALS	50	100	60	100	50	100

7. Which of the following is the third highest cause of accidents for all three locations? 7.____
   A. Severe Weather   B. Impaired Driving
   C. Miscellaneous   D. Excessive Speeding

8. The average number of Severe Weather accidents per week at Location 3 for the year (52 weeks) was MOST NEARLY 8.____
   A. 0.57   B. 30   C. 1   D. 1.25

9. Which location had the LARGEST percentage of accidents caused by Impaired Driving? 9.____
   A. 1   B. 2   C. 3   D. Both A and B

10. If one-third of the accidents at all three locations resulted in at least one fatality, what is the LEAST amount of deaths caused by accidents last year? 10.____
    A. 60   B. 106   C. 66   D. 53

11. What is the percentage of accidents caused by miscellaneous means from all three locations in 2014? 11.____
    A. 5%   B. 10%   C. 13%   D. 25%

12. How many pairs of the following groups of letters are exactly alike? 12.____
    ACDOBJ   ACDBOJ
    HEWBWR   HEWRWB
    DEERVS   DEERVS
    BRFQSX   BRFQSX
    WEYRVB   WEYRVB
    SPQRZA   SQRPZA

    A. 2   B. 3   C. 4   D. 5

Questions 13-19.

DIRECTIONS: Questions 13 through 19 are to be answered on the basis of the following information.

In 2012, the most current information on the American population was finished. The information was compiled by 200 volunteers in each of the 50 states. The territory of Puerto Rico, a sovereign of the United States, had 25 people assigned to compile data. In February of 2010, volunteers in each state and sovereign began collecting information. In Puerto Rico, data collection finished by January 31st, 2011, while work in the United States was completed on June 30, 2012. Each volunteer gathered data on the population of their state or sovereign. When the information was compiled, volunteers sent reports to the nation's capital, Washington, D.C. Each volunteer worked 20 hours per month and put together 10 reports per month. After the data was compiled in total, 50 people reviewed the data and worked from January 2012 to December 2012.

13. How many reports were generated from February 2010 to April 2010 in Illinois and Ohio?
    A. 3,000   B. 6,000   C. 12,000   D. 15,000   13.____

14. How many volunteers in total collected population data in January 2012?
    A. 10,000   B. 2,000   C. 225   D. 200   14.____

15. How many reports were put together in May 2012?
    A. 2,000   B. 50,000   C. 100,000   D. 100,250   15.____

16. How many hours did the Puerto Rican volunteers work in the fall (September-November)?
    A. 60   B. 500   C. 1,500   D. 0   16.____

17. How many workers were compiling or reviewing data in July 2012?
    A. 25   B. 50   C. 200   D. 250   17.____

18. What was the total amount of hours worked by Nevada volunteers in July 2010?
    A. 500   B. 4,000   C. 4,500   D. 5,000   18.____

19. How many reviewers worked in January 2013?
    A. 75   B. 50   C. 0   D. 25   19.____

20. John has to file 10 documents per shelf. How many documents would it take for John to fill 40 shelves?
    A. 40   B. 400   C. 4,500   D. 5,000   20.____

21. Jill wants to travel from New York City to Los Angeles by bike, which is approximately 2,772 miles. How many miles per day would Jill need to average if she wanted to complete the trip in 4 weeks?
    A. 100   B. 89   C. 99   D. 94   21.____

22. If there are 24 CPU's and only 7 monitors, how many more monitors do you need to have the same amount of monitors as CPU's?
    A. Not enough information
    B. 17
    C. 31
    D. 0

    22._____

23. If Gerry works 5 days a week and 8 hours each day, and John works 3 days a week and 10 hours each day, how many more hours per year will Gerry work than John?
    A. They work the same amount of hours.
    B. 450
    C. 520
    D. 832

    23._____

24. Jimmy gets transferred to a new office. The new office has 25 employees, but only 16 are there due to a blizzard. How many coworkers was Jimmy able to meet on his first day?
    A. 16   B. 25   C. 9   D. 7

    24._____

25. If you do a fundraiser for charities in your area and raise $500 total, how much would you give to each charity if you were donating equal amounts to 3 of them?
    A. $250.00   B. $167.77   C. $50.00   D. $111.11

    25._____

KEY (CORRECT ANSWERS)

1.	D		11.	C
2.	B		12.	B
3.	A		13.	C
4.	C		14.	A
5.	D		15.	C
6.	B		16.	C
7.	D		17.	B
8.	A		18.	B
9.	A		19.	C
10.	D		20.	B

21.	C
22.	B
23.	C
24.	A
25.	B

TEST 3

DIRECTIONS: Each question or incomplete statement is followed by several suggested answers or completions. Select the one that BEST answers the question or completes the statement. *PRINT THE LETTER OF THE CORRECT ANSWER IN THE SPACE AT THE RIGHT.*

Questions 1-3.

DIRECTIONS: In answering Questions 1 through 3, choose the correctly spelled word.

1. A. allusion   B. alusion   C. allusien   D. allution   1.____

2. A. altitude   B. alltitude   C. atlitude   D. altlitude   2.____

3. A. althogh   B. allthough   C. althrough   D. although   3.____

Questions 4-9.

DIRECTIONS: In answering Questions 4 through 9, choose the answer that BEST completes the analogy.

4. Odometer is to mileage as compass is to   4.____
   A. speed   B. needle   C. hiking   D. direction

5. Marathon is to race as hibernation is to   5.____
   A. winter   B. dream   C. sleep   D. bear

6. Cup is to coffee as bowl is to   6.____
   A. dish   B. spoon   C. food   D. soup

7. Flow is to river as stagnant is to   7.____
   A. pool   B. rain   C. stream   D. canal

8. Paw is to cat as hoof is to   8.____
   A. lamb   B. horse   C. lion   D. elephant

9. Architect is to building as sculptor is to   9.____
   A. museum   B. chisel   C. stone   D. statue

Questions 10-14.

DIRECTIONS: Questions 10 through 14 are to be answered on the basis of the following graph.

Population of Carroll City Broken Down by Age and Gender (in Thousands)			
Age	Female	Male	Total
Under 15	60	60	120
15-23		22	
24-33		20	44
34-43	13	18	31
44-53	20		67
64 and Over	65	65	130
TOTAL	230	232	462

10. How many people in the city are between the ages of 15-23?
 A. 70 B. 46,000 C. 70,000 D. 225,000

10._____

11. Approximately what percentage of the total population of the city was female aged 24-33?
 A. 10% B. 5% C. 15% D. 25%

11._____

12. If 33% of the males have a job and 55% of females don't have a job, which of the following statements is TRUE?
 A. Males have approximately 2,600 more jobs than females.
 B. Females have approximately 49,000 more jobs than males.
 C. Females have approximately 26,000 more jobs than males.
 D. None of the above statements are true.

12._____

13. How many females between the ages of 15-23 live in Carroll City?
 A. 67,000 B. 24,000 C. 48,000 D. 91,000

13._____

14. Assume all males 44-53 living in Carroll City are employed. If two-thirds of males age 44-53 work jobs outside of Carroll City, how many work within city limits?
 A. 31,333
 B. 15,667
 C. 47,000
 D. Cannot answer the question with the information provided

14._____

Questions 15-16.

DIRECTIONS: Questions 15 and 16 are labeled as shown. Alphabetize them for filing. Choose the answer that correctly shows the order.

15. (1) AED
    (2) OOS
    (3) FOA
    (4) DOM
    (5) COB

    A. 2-5-4-3-2   B. 1-4-5-2-3   C. 1-5-4-2-3   D. 1-5-4-3-2

15.____

16. Alphabetize the names of the people. Last names are given last.
    (1) Lindsey Jamestown
    (2) Jane Alberta
    (3) Ally Jamestown
    (4) Allison Johnston
    (5) Lyle Moreno

    A. 2-1-3-4-5   B. 3-4-2-1-5   C. 2-3-1-4-5   D. 4-3-2-1-5

16.____

17. Which of the following words is misspelled?
    A. disgust   B. whisper
    C. locale   D. none of the above

17.____

Questions 18-21.

DIRECTIONS: Questions 18 through 21 are to be answered on the basis of the following list of employees.

    Robertson, Aaron
    Bacon, Gina
    Jerimiah, Trace
    Gillette, Stanley
    Jacks, Sharon

18. Which employee name would come in third in alphabetized list?
    A. Robertson, Aaron   B. Jerimiah, Trace
    C. Gillette, Stanley   D. Jacks, Sharon

18.____

19. Which employee's first name starts with the letter in the alphabet that is five letters after the first letter of their last name?
    A. Jerimiah, Trace   B. Bacon, Gina
    C. Jacks, Sharon   D. Gillette, Stanley

19.____

20. How many employees have last names that are exactly five letters long?
    A. 1   B. 2   C. 3   D. 4

20.____

21. How many of the employees have either a first or last name that starts with the letter "G"?   21.____
    A. 1   B. 2   C. 4   D. 5

Questions 22-25.

DIRECTIONS: Questions 22 through 25 are to be answered on the basis of the following chart.

Bicycle Sales (Model #34JA32)							
Country	May	June	July	August	September	October	Total
Germany	34	47	45	54	56	60	296
Britain	40	44	36	47	47	46	260
Ireland	37	32	32	32	34	33	200
Portugal	14	14	14	16	17	14	89
Italy	29	29	28	31	29	31	177
Belgium	22	24	24	26	25	23	144
Total	176	198	179	206	208	207	1166

22. What percentage of the overall total was sold to the German importer?   22.____
    A. 25.3%   B. 22%   C. 24.1%   D. 23%

23. What percentage of the overall total was sold in September?   23.____
    A. 24.1%   B. 25.6%   C. 17.9%   D. 24.6%

24. What is the average number of units per month imported into Belgium over the first four months shown?   24.____
    A. 26   B. 20   C. 24   D. 31

25. If you look at the three smallest importers, what is their total import percentage?   25.____
    A. 35.1%   B. 37.1%   C. 40%   D. 28%

KEY (CORRECT ANSWERS)

1.	A		11.	B
2.	A		12.	C
3.	D		13.	C
4.	D		14.	B
5.	C		15.	D
6.	D		16.	C
7.	A		17.	D
8.	B		18.	D
9.	D		19.	B
10.	C		20.	B

21. B
22. A
23. C
24. C
25. A

TEST 4

DIRECTIONS: Each question or incomplete statement is followed by several suggested answers or completions. Select the one that BEST answers the question or completes the statement. *PRINT THE LETTER OF THE CORRECT ANSWER IN THE SPACE AT THE RIGHT.*

Questions 1-6.

DIRECTIONS: In answering Questions 1 through 6, choose the sentence that represents the BEST example of English grammar.

1. A. Joey and me want to go on a vacation next week.
   B. Gary told Jim he would need to take some time off.
   C. If turning six years old, Jim's uncle would teach Spanish to him.
   D. Fax a copy of your resume to Ms. Perez and me.

   1._____

2. A. Jerry stood in line for almost two hours.
   B. The reaction to my engagement was less exciting than I thought it would be.
   C. Carlos and me have done great work on this project.
   D. Two parts of the speech needs to be revised before tomorrow.

   2._____

3. A. Arriving home, the alarm was tripped.
   B. Jonny is regarded as a stand up guy, a responsible parent, and he doesn't give up until a task is finished.
   C. Each employee must submit a drug test each month.
   D. One of the documents was incinerated in the explosion.

   3._____

4. A. As soon as my parents get home, I told them I finished all of my chores.
   B. I asked my teacher to send me my missing work, check my absences, and how did I do on my test.
   C. Matt attempted to keep it concealed from Jenny and me.
   D. If Mary or him cannot get work done on time, I will have to split them up.

   4._____

5. A. Driving to work, the traffic report warned him of an accident on Highway 47.
   B. Jimmy has performed well this season.
   C. Since finishing her degree, several job offers have been given to Cam.
   D. Our boss is creating unstable conditions for we employees.

   5._____

6. A. The thief was described as a tall man with a wiry mustache weighing approximately 150 pounds.
   B. She gave Patrick and I some more time to finish our work.
   C. One of the books that he ordered was damaged in shipping.
   D. While talking on the rotary phone, the car Jim was driving skidded off the road.

   6._____

Questions 7-9.

DIRECTIONS: Questions 7 through 9 are to be answered on the basis of the following graph.

Ice Lake Frozen Flight (2002-2013)		
Year	Number of Participants	Temperature (Fahrenheit)
2002	22	4°
2003	50	33°
2004	69	18°
2005	104	22°
2006	108	24°
2007	288	33°
2008	173	9°
2009	598	39°
2010	698	26°
2011	696	30°
2012	777	28°
2013	578	32°

7. Which two year span had the LARGEST difference between temperatures?
   A. 2002 and 2003
   B. 2011 and 2012
   C. 2008 and 2009
   D. 2003 and 2004

8. How many total people participated in the years after the temperature reached at least 29°?
   A. 2,295   B. 1,717   C. 2,210   D. 4,543

9. In 2007, the event saw 288 participants, while in 2008 that number dropped to 173. Which of the following reasons BEST explains the drop in participants?
   A. The event had not been going on that long and people didn't know about it.
   B. The lake water wasn't cold enough to have people jump in.
   C. The temperature was too cold for many people who would have normally participated.
   D. None of the above reasons explain the drop in participants.

10. In the following list of numbers, how many times does 4 come just after 2 when 2 comes just after an odd number?
    2365247653898632488572486392424
    A. 2   B. 3   C. 4   D. 5

11. Which choice below lists the letter that is as far after B as S is after N in the alphabet?
    A. G   B. H   C. I   D. J

Questions 12-15.

DIRECTIONS: Questions 12 through 15 are to be answered on the basis of the following directory and list of changes.

Directory		
Name	Emp. Type	Position
Julie Taylor	Warehouse	Packer
James King	Office	Administrative Assistant
John Williams	Office	Salesperson
Ray Moore	Warehouse	Maintenance
Kathleen Byrne	Warehouse	Supervisor
Amy Jones	Office	Salesperson
Paul Jonas	Office	Salesperson
Lisa Wong	Warehouse	Loader
Eugene Lee	Office	Accountant
Bruce Lavine	Office	Manager
Adam Gates	Warehouse	Packer
Will Suter	Warehouse	Packer
Gary Lorper	Office	Accountant
Jon Adams	Office	Salesperson
Susannah Harper	Office	Salesperson

Directory Updates:
- Employee e-mail addresses will adhere to the following guidelines: lastnamefirstname@apexindustries.com (ex. Susannah Harper is harpersusannah@apexindustries.com). Currently, employees in the warehouse share one e-mail, distribution@apexindustries.com.
- The "Loader" position will now be referred to as "Specialist I"
- Adam Gates has accepted a Supervisor position within the Warehouse and is no longer a Packer. All warehouse employees report to the two Supervisors and all office employees report to the Manager.

12. Amy Jones tried to send an e-mail to Adam Gates, but it wouldn't send. Which of the following offers the BEST explanation?
    A. Amy put Adam's first name first and then his last name.
    B. Adam doesn't check his e-mail, so he wouldn't know if he received the e-mail or not.
    C. Adam does not have his own e-mail.
    D. Office employees are not allowed to send e-mails to each other.

12.____

13. How many Packers currently work for Apex Industries?
    A. 2   B. 3   C. 4   D. 5

13.____

14. What position does Lisa Wong currently hold?
    A. Specialist I   B. Secretary
    C. Administrative Assistant   D. Loader

14.____

15. If an employee wanted to contact the office manager, which of the following e-mails should the e-mail be sent to?   15.____
    A. officemanager@apexindustries.com
    B. brucelavine@apexindustries.com
    C. lavinebruce@apexindustries.com
    D. distribution@apexindustries.com

Questions 16-19.

DIRECTIONS: In answering Questions 16 through 19, compare the three names, numbers or addresses.

16. Smiley Yarnell   Smiley Yarnel   Smily Yarnell   16.____
    A. All three are exactly alike.
    B. The first and second are exactly alike.
    C. The second and third are exactly alike.
    D. All three are different.

17. 1583 Theater Drive   1583 Theater Drive   1583 Theatre Drive   17.____
    A. All three are exactly alike.
    B. The first and second are exactly alike.
    C. The second and third are exactly alike.
    D. All three are different.

18. 3341893212   3341893212   3341893212   18.____
    A. All three are exactly alike.
    B. The first and second are exactly alike.
    C. The second and third are exactly alike.
    D. All three are different.

19. Douglass Watkins   Douglas Watkins   Douglass Watkins   19.____
    A. All three are exactly alike.
    B. The first and third are exactly alike.
    C. The second and third are exactly alike.
    D. All three are different.

Questions 20-24.

DIRECTIONS: In answering Questions 20 through 24, you will be presented with a word. Choose the synonym that BEST represents the word in question.

20. Flexible   20.____
    A. delicate   B. inflammable   C. strong   D. pliable

21. Alternative   21.____
    A. choice   B. moderate   C. lazy   D. value

22. Corroborate
    A. examine   B. explain   C. verify   D. explain

23. Respiration
    A. recovery   B. breathing   C. sweating   D. selfish

24. Negligent
    A. lazy   B. moderate   C. hopeless   D. lax

25. Plumber is to Wrench as Painter is to
    A. pipe   B. shop   C. hammer   D. brush

KEY (CORRECT ANSWERS)

1. D
2. A
3. D
4. C
5. B

6. C
7. C
8. B
9. C
10. C

11. A
12. C
13. A
14. A
15. C

16. D
17. B
18. A
19. B
20. D

21. A
22. C
23. B
24. D
25. D

GLOSSARY OF COMPUTER TERMS

Basic

accessibility
The term accessibility refers to information that can be accessed with fewer or no obstacles for as many people as possible. Developers use accessibility features in websites and software to benefit users with disabilities to use computers through assistive technologies.

artificial intelligence
Artificial intelligence or AI is the ability of a computer to perform tasks related to intelligence and think like humans. This technology can process large amounts of data to recognize patterns and make decisions like humans, as seen in programs like ChatGPT.

API
Also called application programming interface, API is a set of protocols and instructions (written in C++ or JavaScript) to determine how two software components will communicate with each other. It defines the kinds of calls and requests made to locate and retrieve the requested information.

application (app)
An application (often called "app" for short) is a computer program that performs specific functions for an end user or another application (in some cases).

authentication
The process of verification of a user or device before allowing access to the system or resources.

bandwidth
A measurement of the amount of data that can be transmitted over a communications path in a given time. The higher the bandwidth, the greater the volume of data transmitted. It is usually measured in bits per second (bps). Modern networks have speed that is measured in the millions of bits per second (megabits per second, or Mbps) or billions of bits per second (gigabits per second, or Gbps).

blockchain
Blockchain technology is an advanced database mechanism that enables the secure sharing of information. It is also known as distributed ledger technology or DLT. The data is stored in blocks that are lined together in a chain.

boot
Starting up an OS is booting it. If the computer is already running, it is more often called rebooting.

browser
A browser is a program used to browse the web. Some common browsers include Google Chrome, Microsoft Edge, Mozilla Firefox, Brave and Safari.

bug
A bug is a mistake in the design of something, especially software. A really severe bug can cause something to crash.

BYOD
Bring Your Own Device or BYOD is a business policy allowing employees to bring in their personal devices and use them to access company data, e-mail and other resources.

Business Intelligence
Business intelligence or BI is a tool that is used by businesses for data collection, analysis and presentation in a meaningful way to drive the decision-making process.

CAPTCHA
Acronym for Completely Automated Public Turing test to tell Computers and Humans Apart. It is

a test in form of distorted text or images that determines if an online user is really a human or an automated user.

cache
A software or hardware component that temporarily stores data in a computing environment to reduce the data retrieval time for future requests.

chatbot
A chat bot or chatterbox is a computer program that is used for simulating and processing human conversation. It is a form of artificial intelligence (AI) that allows humans to interact with digital devices as if they were communicating with a real person.

chat
Chatting is like e-mail, only it is done instantaneously and can directly involve multiple people at once. Chat is a kind of communication over the Internet that allows real-time transmission of messages between sender and receiver. Chat messages are short to enable the participants to respond quickly.

click
To press a mouse button. When done twice in rapid succession, it is referred to as a double-click.

cloud computing
Refers to storage and access data and programs over the Internet instead of any hard drive. Some common cloud services include Dropbox, iCloud and Google Cloud.

cookie
A piece of data from a website stored within a web browser that a website can retrieve at a later time. It is used throughout a user's session to keep track of usage patterns and preferences.

cursor
A point of attention on the computer screen, often marked with a flashing line or block. Text typed into the computer will usually appear at the cursor.

cybercrime
An illegal activity that involves a network or computer. Some common cybercrimes include identity theft, gaining unauthorized access and network intrusions.

cybersecurity
Measures that are designed to protect information, computer devices or networks from cybercrime.

cyberspace
The world of virtual computers, specifically electronic media, used to facilitate online communication.

data center
A physical facility that is used to house an organization's applications and data. The key components of a data center design include servers, storage systems, firewalls, routers, switches and application-delivery controllers.

database
A database is a collection of data, typically organized to make common retrievals easy and efficient. Some common database programs include Oracle, Sybase, Postgres, Mango DB, Microsoft SQL Server, Redis, Filemaker, Adabas, etc.

decryption
It is the process of converting an encrypted message back to its original form. It is the reverse process of encryption.

desktop
A desktop system is a computer designed to sit in one position on a desk somewhere and not move around. Most general-purpose computers are desktop systems. Calling a system a desktop implies nothing about its platform. Industrial desktop systems are typically called workstations.

directory
Also called "folder," a directory is a collection of files typically created for organizational

purposes. Note that a directory is itself a file, so a directory can generally contain other directories. It differs in this way from a partition.

disk

A disk is a physical object used for storing data. It will not forget its data when it loses power. It is always used in conjunction with a disk drive. Some disks can be removed from their drives, some cannot. Generally it is possible to write new information to a disk in addition to reading data from it, but this is not always the case.

drive

A device for storing and/or retrieving data. Some drives (such as disk drives, zip drives, and tape drives) are typically capable of having new data written to them, but some others (like CD-ROMs or DVD-ROMs) are not. Some drives have random access (like disk drives, zip drives, CD-ROMs, and DVD-ROMs), while others only have sequential access (like tape drives).

e-book

An e-book or electronic book is a digital and non-editable text that is available and displayed on electronic devices (smartphone or tablets). The concept behind an e-book is that it should provide all the functionality of an ordinary book but in a manner that is (overall) less expensive and more environmentally friendly. The actual term e-book is somewhat confusingly used to refer to a variety of things: custom software to play e-book titles, dedicated hardware to play e-book titles, and the e-book titles themselves. Individual e-book titles can be free or commercial (but will always be less expensive than their printed counterparts) and have to be loaded into a player to be read. Players vary wildly in capability level. Basic ones allow simple reading and bookmarking; better ones include various features like hypertext, illustrations, audio, and even limited video. Other optional features allow the user to mark-up sections of text, leave notes, circle or diagram things, highlight passages, program or customize settings, and even use interactive fiction.

email

Email is short for electronic mail. It allows for the transfer of information from one user to others, provided they are hooked up via some sort of network Popular email platforms include Gmail and Yahoo.

encryption

The process of data conversion from readable form into encoded form is called encryption. It is used to hide sensitive information and prevent unauthorized access.

end point

Physical devices that are connected to a computer network such as servers, mobile devices, desktop computers and virtual machines.

end user

An individual who will ultimately use an IT product or service.

file

A file is a unit of (usually named) information stored on a computer.

firewall

A network security device that acts as a barrier to monitor and filter incoming and outgoing network traffic and permits/blocks data packets based on previously established security policies.

firmware

Sort of in-between hardware and software, firmware consists of modifiable programs embedded in hardware. Firmware updates should be treated with care since they can literally destroy the underlying hardware if done improperly. There are also cases where neglecting to apply a firmware update can destroy the underlying hardware, so user beware. Cameras, optical drives, printers, mobile phones, network cards, etc. rely on firmware built into their memory for smooth functioning.

floppy

A once-common type of removable disk. Floppy disks did not hold much data, but most computers were capable of reading them. They typically held 100 KB to 1.44 MB of data.

format

The manner in which data is stored; its organization. For example, VHS, SVHS, and Beta are three different formats of video tape. They are not 100% compatible with each other, but information can be transferred from one to the other with the proper equipment (but not always without loss; SVHS contains more information than either of the other two). Computer information can be stored in literally hundreds of different formats, and can represent text, sounds, graphics, animations, etc. Computer information can be exchanged via different computer types provided both computers can interpret the format used.

freeware

A type of proprietary software that is available for downloading without charge. Depending on the freeware's copyright, the user may or may not reuse the software.

function keys

On a computer keyboard, the keys that start with an "F" and usually (but not always) found on the top row. They are meant to perform user-defined tasks.

GPS

GPS or Global Positioning System is a radio-based global navigation satellite system that allows the user to determine a location on Earth.

graphics

Anything visually displayed on a computer that is not text.

GUI

A graphical user interface (GUI) is a digital interface through which a user interacts with electronic devices (smartphones, computers) with graphical components such as icons, menus, buttons and other visual indicators. GUI representations are manipulated by mouse, touch screen, finger, stylus, or trackball.

hardware

The physical portion of the computer.

help desk

A help desk is an information and assistance resource that provides technical support for hardware or software. Companies provide help desk support to their customers via a toll-free number, e-mail or website. The goal of a help desk is to help customers troubleshoot issues and guide them to navigate technology properly.

hypertext

A hypertext document is like a text document with the ability to contain pointers to other regions of (possibly other) hypertext documents.

IaaS

Infrastructure as a Service (IaaS) is the most basic cloud-service model that offers computing, storage and networking resources on demand and pay-as-you-go basis.

Internet

The Internet is the world-wide network of computers.

IoT

Internet of Things (IoT) refers to the collective network of connected devices and the technology that facilitates communication between devices and the cloud. IoT includes anything with a sensor that is assigned a unique identifier (UID).

IT infrastructure

Systems that are put in place to facilitate operation and management of IT services and environments. There are two types of IT infrastructure: traditional infrastructure and cloud infrastructure.

keyboard

A keyboard on a computer is almost identical to a keyboard on a typewriter. Computer keyboards will typically have extra keys, however. Some of these keys (common examples include Control, Alt, and Fn) are meant to be used in conjunction with other keys just like shift on a regular typewriter. Other keys (common examples include Insert, Delete, Home, End, Help, function keys,etc.) are meant to be used independently and often perform editing tasks. Keyboards on different platforms will often look slightly different and have somewhat different collections of keys.

LAN
A local area network (LAN) is a group of connected computing devices that usually share a centralized Internet connection. A LAN may serve 2-3 users in a home or thousands of users in a central office.

language
Computer programs can be written in a variety of different languages. Different languages are optimized for different tasks. Common languages include JavaScript, Python, C#, Rust, Kotlin, Swift, Go and Elixir. Some people classify languages into two categories, higher-level and lower-level. These people would consider assembly language and machine language lower-level languages and all other languages higher-level. In general, higher-level languages can be either interpreted or compiled; many languages allow both, but some are restricted to one or the other. Many people do not consider machine language and assembly language at all when talking about programming languages.

laptop
A laptop is any computer designed for portability with the capability to do most of the same functions as a desktop system. They are battery-powered and typically provide several hours of use between charges. Most laptops run Windows or Apple operating systems, though Google's Chromebook laptop has gained in popularity.

learning management system (LMS)
Software that is developed to create, use, manage, deliver and store online training course content for audience. The primary purpose of an LMS is to simplify the learning process for the organization and keep the knowledge of an audience up to date.

machine learning (ML)
A branch of artificial intelligence (AI) that uses data and algorithms to improve the performance of AI to imitate intelligent human behavior.

malware
Malware, also referred to as malicious software, is a program or file that is designed to disrupt computer systems, networks or servers. Some common types of malware include viruses, worms, Trojan horses, ransomware and spyware.

mail server
A mail server is a dedicated software program that supports electronic mail. It stores incoming mail for distribution to users and forwards outgoing mail. Some common mail servers include Microsoft Exchange, iCloud Mail and Sendmail.

memory
Computer memory is used to temporarily store data. In reality, computer memory is only capable of remembering sequences of zeros and ones, but by utilizing the binary number system it is possible to produce arbitrary rational numbers and through clever formatting all manner of representations of pictures, sounds, and animations. The most common types of memory are RAM, ROM, and flash.

MHz & megahertz
One megahertz is equivalent to 1000 kilohertz, or 1,000,000 hertz. The clock speed of the main processor of many computers is measured in MHz, and is sometimes (quite misleadingly) used to represent the overall speed of a computer. In fact, a computer's speed is based upon many factors, and since MHz only reveals how many clock cycles the main processor has per second (saying nothing about how much is actually accomplished per cycle), it can really only accurately be used to gauge two computers with the same generation and family of processor plus similar configurations of memory, co-processors, and other peripheral hardware.

modem
A modem allows two computers to communicate over ordinary phone lines. It derives its name from modulate / demodulate, the process by which it converts digital computer data back and forth for use with an analog phone line.

monitor
The screen for viewing computer information is called a monitor.

mouse
In computer parlance a mouse can be both the physical object moved around to control a pointer on the screen, and the pointer itself.

multimedia
This originally indicated a capability to work with and integrate various types of things including audio, still graphics, and especially video. Now it is more of a marketing term and has little real meaning.

NC
The term network computer refers to any (usually desktop) computer system that is designed to work as part of a network rather than as a stand-alone machine. This saves money on hardware, software, and maintenance by taking advantage of facilities already available on the network. The term "Internet appliance" is often used interchangeably with NC.

network
A network (as applied to computers) typically means a group of computers working together. It can also refer to the physical wires connecting the computers.

notebook
A notebook is a small laptop with similar price, performance, and battery life.

organizer
An organizer is a tiny computer used primarily to store names, addresses, phone numbers, and date book information. They usually have some ability to exchange information with desktop systems. They are extremely inexpensive but are typically incapable of running any special-purpose applications and are thus of limited use.

OS (Operating System)
The operating system is the program that manages a computer's resources. Commonly used OSs include Ubuntu, Windows, MacOS, Android, and Google ChromeOS.

PaaS
Platform as a Service (PaaS) is a cloud computing model that provides a computing platform including hardware, software, and infrastructure for development, running and management of applications. PaaS frees the developers to install in-house hardware and software to develop or run a new application.

PC
The term personal computer properly refers to any desktop, laptop, or notebook computer system. Its use is inconsistent, though, and some use it to specifically refer Windows-based computers.

PDA
A personal digital assistant is a predecessor of mobile phones and smartphones. It is a small battery-powered computer intended to be carried around by the user rather than left on a desk. It is used to carry out certain functions, including scheduling, organization, translation, etc. PDAs largely became obsolete with the advance and improvement of mobile-phone technology.

phishing
A common type of cyberattack that targets victims through phone calls, email, text messages or other forms of communication. This attack aims to trick the receiver by posing as a trustworthy entity to obtain sensitive information such as credit card details, personally identifiable information and login credentials.

platform
Roughly speaking, a platform represents a computer's family. It is defined by both the processor

type on the hardware side and the OS type on the software side. Computers belonging to different platforms cannot typically run each other's programs (unless the programs are written in a language like Java).

portable
If something is portable it can be easily moved from one type of computer to another. The verb "to port" indicates the moving itself.

printer
A printer is a piece of hardware that will print computer information onto paper.

processor
The processor (also called central processing unit, or CPU) is the part of the computer that actually works with the data and runs the programs. There are two main processor types in common usage today: CISC and RISC. Some computers have more than one processor and are thus called "multiprocessor". This is distinct from multitasking. Advertisers often use megahertz numbers as a means of showing a processor's speed. This is often extremely misleading; megahertz numbers are more or less meaningless when compared across different types of processors.

program
A program is a series of instructions for a computer, telling it what to do or how to behave. The terms "application" and "app" mean almost the same thing (albeit applications generally have GUIs). It is however different from an applet. Program is also the verb that means to create a program, and a programmer is one who programs.

run
Running a program is how it is made to do something. The term "execute" means the same thing.

SaaS
Software as a Service (SaaS) is a cloud-based software delivery model that delivers applications over the Internet. SaaS enables companies to use software on-promise without worrying about installing, renewing and maintaining them.

search engine
A software program or tool that enables the users to search information on the internet. It creates indexes of databases based on titles of files, keywords or full text of files. Google, Baidu and Yahoo are some popular search engines.

SEO
SEO or search engine optimization is the process and practice of improving various aspects of a website to increase its visibility in search engines.

software
The non-physical portion of the computer; the part that exists only as data; the programs. Another term meaning much the same is "code."

spam
Use of electronic messaging systems to send unwanted bulk messages. Different types of spam include phishing emails, email spoofing, tech support scams, malspam, spam calls and spam texts.

spreadsheet
A program used to perform various calculations. It is especially popular for financial applications. Some common spreadsheets include Microsoft Excel and Google Sheets.

Trojan horse
A Trojan horse or Trojan is a type of malware that is designed to disguise itself as legitimate code to perform harmful acts. Once it is inside the network, the attacker can carry out any action that legitimate user could perform such as deleting files, modifying data, exporting files, etc.

troubleshooting
The process of providing technical support that includes identification, planning and resolution of problems, faults or errors within the computer system or software.

user
The operator of a computer.

virtual machine
A virtual machine or VM is a computer resource that is not physical. It uses software instead of a physical computer for running programs and deploying applications. VM software can run operating systems, connect to networks, store data and perform other computational functions. Some popular VM include VMware Workstation, VirtualBox, QEMU, Citrix and VMWare Fusion.

VPN
A virtual private network (VPN) is an encrypted internet connection. A VPN hides actual public IP addresses of the user and tunnels the traffic between user's device and the remote server. The aim of using VPN is to ensure sensitive data is safely transmitted.

WAN
A wide area network or WAN is a type of network that exists over a large geographical area.

Wi-Fi
A wireless technology using radio waves to provide high-speed Internet access.

word processor
A program designed to help with the production of textual documents, like letters and memos. Heavier duty work can be done with a desktop publisher. Some common word processors include Microsoft Word and Google Docs.

workstation
A workstation is an individual computer or group of computers that are used by a single user to accomplish professional tasks. Workstations are useful for development and applications that need moderate amount of computing power and high-quality graphics.

www
The World-Wide-Web refers more or less to all the publicly accessible documents on the Internet. It is used quite loosely, and sometimes indicates only HTML files and sometimes FTP and Gopher files, too. It is also sometimes just referred to as "the web".

Reference

The following are past and present elements of computing and computer systems, to be reviewed for reference purposes. In some cases, the element is no longer relevant to modern computing but is important for the study and understanding of previous computing environments.

a11y
Commonly used to abbreviate the word "accessibility." There are eleven letters between the "a" and the "y".

ADA
An object-oriented language at one point popular for military and some academic software.

AIX
The industrial strength OS designed by IBM to run on PowerPC and x86 based machines. It was a variant of UNIX and was meant to provide more power than OS/2.

AJaX
AJaX is a little like DHTML, but it adds asynchronous communication between the browser and Web site via either XML or JSON to achieve performance that often rivals desktop applications.

AltiVec
AltiVec (also called the "Velocity Engine") was a special extension built into some PowerPC CPUs to provide better performance for certain operations, most notably graphics and sound. It was similar to MMX on the x86 CPUs. Like MMX, it required special software for full performance benefits to be realized.

Amiga
A platform originally created and only produced by Commodore and later owned by Gateway 2000 and produced by it and a few smaller companies. It was historically the first multimedia machine and gave the world of computing many innovations. Many music videos were created on Amigas, and a few television series and movies had their special effects generated on Amigas. Also, Amigas were readily synchronized with video cameras, so typically when a computer screen appears on television or in a movie and it is not flickering wildly, it is probably an Amiga in disguise. Many coin-operated arcade games were really Amigas packaged in stand-up boxes.

AmigaOS
The OS used by Amigas. AmigaOS combined the functionality of an OS and a window manager and was fully multitasking. AmigaOS boasted a pretty good selection of games (many arcade games are in fact written on Amigas) but had limited driver support. AmigaOS ran on 68xx, Alpha, and PowerPC based machines.

Apple II
The Apple II computer sold millions of units and is generally considered to have been the first home computer with a 1977 release date. It is based on the 65xx family of processors. The earlier Apple I was only available as a build-it-yourself kit.

AppleScript
A scripting language for Mac OS computers. It is used for basic calculations, text processing and processing complex tasks.

applet
An applet differs from an application in that is not meant to be run stand-alone but rather with the assistance of another program, usually a browser.

Aqua
The default window manager for Mac OS X.

Archie
Archie was a system for searching through FTP archives for particular files. It tends not to be used too much anymore as more general modern search engines are significantly more capable.

ARM
An ARM is a RISC processor invented by Advanced RISC Machines. ARMs are different from most other processors in that they were not designed to maximize speed but rather to maximize speed per power consumed. Thus ARMs found most of their use on hand-held machines and PDAs. A few different OSes run on ARM based machines including Newton OS, JavaOS, Windows CE and Linux. The Cortex-X4 is the fastest ARM CPU ever built.

ASCII
The ASCII character set is the most popular one in common use. People will often refer to a bare text file without complicated embedded format instructions as an ASCII file, and such files can usually be transferred from one computer system to another with relative ease. Unfortunately, there are a few minor variations of it that pop up here and there, and if you receive a text file that seems subtly messed up with punctuation marks altered or upper and lower case reversed, you are probably encountering one of the ASCII variants. It is usually fairly straightforward to translate from one ASCII variant to another, though. The ASCII character set is seven bit while pure binary is usually eight bit, so transferring a binary file through ASCII channels will result in corruption and loss of data. Note also that the ASCII character set is a subset of the Unicode character set.

ASK
A protocol for an infrared communications port on a device. It predates the IrDA compliant infrared communications protocol and is not compatible with it. Many devices with infrared communications support both, but some only support one or the other.

assembly language
Assembly language is essentially machine language that has had some of the numbers

replaced by somewhat easier to remember mnemonics in an attempt to make it more human-readable. The program that converts assembly language to machine language is called an assembler. While assembly language predates FORTRAN, it is not typically what people think of when they discuss computer languages.

authoring system
Any GUIs method of designing new software can be called an authoring system. Any computer language name with the word "visual" in front of it is probably a version of that language built with some authoring system capabilities.

AWK
AWK is an interpreted language developed in 1977 by Aho, Weinberger, & Kernighan. It gets its name from its creators' initials. It was not particularly fast, but it was designed for creating small throwaway programs rather than full-blown applications -- it is designed to make the writing of the program fast, not the program itself. It was quite portable with versions existing for numerous platforms, including a free GNU version. Plus, virtually every version of UNIX in the world came with AWK built-in.

BASIC
The Beginners' All-purpose Symbolic Instruction Code is a computer language developed by Kemeny & Kurtz in 1964.

baud
A measure of communications speed, used typically for modems indicating how many bits per second can be transmitted.

BBS
A bulletin board system was a computer that could be directly connected to via modem and provided various services like e-mail, chatting, newsgroups, and file downloading. BBSs waned in popularity with the rise of Internet access.

BeOS
A lightweight OS available for both PowerPC and x86 based machines. It is often referred to simply as "Be".

beta
A beta version of something is not yet ready for prime time but still possibly useful to related developers and other interested parties. Expect beta software to crash more than properly released software does. Traditionally beta versions (of commercial software) are distributed only to selected testers who are often then given a discount on the proper version after its release in exchange for their testing work. Beta versions of non-commercial software are more often freely available to anyone who has an interest.

binary
There are two meanings for binary in common computer usage. The first is the name of the number system in which there are only zeros and ones. This is important to computers because all computer data is ultimately a series of zeros and ones, and thus can be represented by binary numbers. The second is an offshoot of the first; data that is not meant to be interpreted through a common character set (like ASCII) is typically referred to as binary data. Pure binary data is typically eight bit data, and transferring a binary file through ASCII channels without prior modification will result in corruption and loss of data. Binary data can be turned into ASCII data via uucoding or bcoding.

bit
A bit can either be on or off; one or zero. All computer data can ultimately be reduced to a series of bits. The term is also used as a (very rough) measure of sound quality, color quality, and even processor capability by considering the fact that series of bits can represent binary numbers. For example (without getting too technical), an eight bit image can contain at most 256 distinct colors while a sixteen bit image can contain at most 65,536 distinct colors.

bitmap
A bitmap is a simplistic representation of an image on a computer, simply indicating whether or

not pixels are on or off, and sometimes indicating their color. Often fonts are represented as bitmaps. The term "pixmap" is sometimes used similarly; typically when a distinction is made, pixmap refers to color images and bitmap refers to monochrome images.

blog
Short for web log, a blog is a website or page containing periodic (usually frequent) posts. Blogs are usually syndicated via either some type of RSS or Atom and often supports TrackBacks. It is not uncommon for blogs to function much like newspaper columns. A blogger is someone who writes for and maintains a blog.

boolean
Boolean algebra is the mathematics of base two numbers. Since base two numbers have only two values, zero and one, there is a good analogy between base two numbers and the logical values "true" & "false". In common usage, booleans are therefore considered to be simple logical values like true & false and the operations that relate them, most typically "and", "or" and "not". Since everyone has a basic understanding of the concepts of true & false and basic conjunctions, everyone also has a basic understanding of boolean concepts -- they just may not realize it.

byte
A byte is a grouping of bits. It is typically eight bits, but there are those who use non-standard byte sizes. Bytes are usually measured in large groups, and the term "kilobyte" (often abbreviated as K) means one-thousand twenty-four (1024) bytes; the term "megabyte" (often abbreviated as M) means one-thousand twenty-four (1024) K; the term gigabyte (often abbreviated as G) means one-thousand twenty-four (1024) M; and the term "terabyte" (often abbreviated as T) means one-thousand twenty-four (1024) G. Memory is typically measured in kilobytes or megabytes, and disk space is typically measured in megabytes or gigabytes. Note that the multipliers here are 1024 instead of the more common 1000 as would be used in the metric system. This is to make it easier to work with the binary number system.

bytecode
Sometimes computer languages that are said to be either interpreted or compiled are in fact neither and are more accurately said to be somewhere in between. Such languages are compiled into bytecode which is then interpreted on the target system. Bytecode tends to be binary but will work on any machine with the appropriate runtime environment (or virtual machine) for it.

C
C is one of the most popular computer languages in the world, and quite possibly *the* most popular. It is a compiled language widely supported on many platforms. It tends to be more portable than FORTRAN but less portable than Java; it has been standardized by ANSI as "ANSI C" -- older versions are called either "K&R C" or "Kernighan and Ritchie C" (in honor of C's creators), or sometimes just "classic C". Fast and simple, it can be applied to all manner of general purpose tasks. C compilers are made by several companies, but the free GNU version (gcc) is still considered one of the best. Newer C-like object-oriented languages include both Java and C++.

C#
C# is a compiled object-oriented language based heavily on C++ with some Java features.

C++
C++ is a compiled object-oriented language. Based heavily on C, C++ is nearly as fast and can often be thought of as being just C with added features. It is currently probably the second most popular object-oriented language, but it has the drawback of being fairly complex -- the much simpler but somewhat slower Java is probably the most popular object-oriented language. Note that C++ was developed independently of the somewhat similar Objective-C; it is however related to Objective-C++.

C64/128
The Commodore 64 computer was a massively successful model of computer with estimated

tens of millions units sold. Its big brother, the Commodore 128, was not quite as popular but still sold several million units. Both units sported ROM-based BASIC and used it as a default "OS". The C128 also came with CP/M (it was a not-often-exercized option on the C64). In their later days they were also packaged with GEOS. Both are based on 65xx family processors.

chain
Some computer devices support chaining, the ability to string multiple devices in a sequence plugged into just one computer port. Often, but not always, such a chain will require some sort of terminator to mark the end. For an example, a SCSI scanner may be plugged into a SCSI CD-ROM drive that is plugged into a SCSI hard drive that is in turn plugged into the main computer. For all these components to work properly, the scanner would also have to have a proper terminator in use. Device chaining has been around a long time, and it is interesting to note that C64/128 serial devices supported it from the very beginning.

character set
Since in reality all a computer can store are series of zeros and ones, representing common things like text takes a little work. The solution is to view the series of zeros and ones instead as a sequence of bytes, and map each one to a particular letter, number, or symbol. The full mapping is called a character set. The most popular character set is commonly referred to as ASCII. The second most popular character set is Unicode

COBOL
The Common Business Oriented Language is a language developed back in 1959. While it was relatively portable, it was disliked by many professional programmers simply because COBOL programs tended to be physically longer than equivalent programs written in almost any other language in common use.

compiled
If a program is compiled, its original human-readable source has been converted into a form more easily used by a computer prior to it being run. Such programs will generally run more quickly than interpreted programs, because time was pre-spent in the compilation phase. A program that compiles other programs is called a compiler.

compression
It is often possible to remove redundant information or capitalize on patterns in data to make a file smaller. Usually when a file has been compressed, it cannot be used until it is uncompressed. Image files are common exceptions, though, as many popular image file formats have compression built-in.

cookie
A cookie is a small file that a web page on another machine writes to your personal machine's disk to store various bits of information. Many people strongly detest cookies and the whole idea of them, and most browsers allow the reception of cookies to be disabled or at least selectively disabled. Sites that maintain shopping carts or remember a reader's last position have legitimate uses for cookies. Sites without such functionality that still spew cookies with distant (or worse, non-existent) expiration dates should perhaps be treated with a little caution.

crash
If a bug in a program is severe enough, it can cause that program to crash, or to become inoperable without being restarted. On machines that are not multitasking, the entire machine will crash and have to be rebooted. On machines that are only partially multitasking the entire machine will sometimes crash and have to be rebooted. On machines that are fully multitasking, the machine should never crash and require a reboot.

crippleware
Crippleware is a variant of shareware that will either self-destruct after its trial period or has built-in limitations to its functionality that get removed after its purchase.

CSS
Cascading style sheets are used in conjunction with HTML and XHTML to define the layout of web pages. While CSS is how current web pages declare how they should be displayed, it

tends not to be supported well (if at all) by ancient browsers.
desktop publisher
A program for creating newspapers, magazines, books, etc. Some common desktop publishing programs include Adobe InDesign, Canva, Affinity Publisher and Microsoft Publisher.
DHTML
Dynamic HTML is simply the combined use of both CSS and JavaScript together in the same document; a more extreme form is called AJaX. Note that DHTML is quite different from the similarly named DTML.
dict
A protocol used for looking up definitions across a network (in particular the Internet).
digital camera
A digital camera looks and behaves like a regular camera, except instead of using film, it stores the image it sees in memory as a file for later transfer to a computer. Many digital cameras offer additional storage besides their own internal memory; a few sport some sort of disk but the majority utilize some sort of flash card. Digital cameras were eventually integrated into mobile phones and are now a dominant element of smartphone technology.
DNS
Domain name service is the means by which a name (like www.saugus.net or ftp.saugus.net) gets converted into a real Internet address that points to a particular machine.
DoS
In a denial of service attack, many individual (usually compromised) computers are used to try and simultaneously access the same public resource with the intent of overburdening it so that it will not be able to adequately serve its normal users.
DOS
A disk operating system manages disks and other system resources. Sort of a subset of OSes, sort of an archaic term for the same. MS-DOS is the most popular program currently calling itself a DOS. CP/M was the most popular prior to MS-DOS.
download
To download a file is to copy it from a remote computer to your own. The opposite is upload.
driver
A driver is a piece of software that works with the OS to control a particular piece of hardware, like a printer, scanner or mouse.
DRM
DRM can stand for either Digital Rights Management or Digital Restrictions Management. In either case, DRM is used to place restrictions upon the usage of digital media ranging from software to music to video.
DTML
The Document Template Mark-up Language is a subset of SGML and a superset of HTML used for creating documents that dynamically adapt to external conditions using its own custom tags and a little bit of Python. Note that it is quite different from the similarly named DHTML.
EDBIC
The EDBIC character set is similar to (but less popular than) the ASCII character set in concept, but is significantly different in layout. It tends to be found only on old machines.
embedded
An embedded system is a computer that lives inside another device and acts as a component of that device. For example, cars have an embedded computer under the hood that helps regulate much of their day-to-day operation. An embedded file lives inside another and acts as a portion of that file. This is frequently seen with HTML files having embedded audio files; audio files often embedded in HTML include AU files, MIDI files, SID files, WAV files, AIFF files, and MOD files. Most browsers will ignore these files unless an appropriate plug-in is present.

emulator
An emulator is a program that allows one computer platform to mimic another for the purposes of running its software. Typically (but not always) running a program through an emulator will not be quite as pleasant an experience as running it on the real system.

environment
An environment (sometimes also called a runtime environment) is a collection of external variable items or parameters that a program can access when run. Information about the computer's hardware and the user can often be found in the environment.

extension
Filename extensions allow a grouping of different file types by putting a tag at the end of the name, such as .doc or .pdf.

FAQ
A frequently asked questions file attempts to provide answers for all commonly asked questions related to a given topic.

FireWire
An incredibly fast type of serial port that offers many of the best features of SCSI at a lower price. Faster than most types of parallel port, a single FireWire port is capable of chaining many devices without the need of a terminator. FireWire is similar in many respects to USB but is significantly faster and somewhat more expensive. It is heavily used for connecting audio/video devices to computers, but is also used for connecting storage devices like drives and other assorted devices like printers and scanners.

fixed width
As applied to a font, fixed width means that every character takes up the same amount of space. That is, an "i" will be just as wide as an "m" with empty space being used for padding. The opposite is variable width. The most common fixed width font is Courier.

flash
Flash memory is similar to RAM. It has one significant advantage: it does not lose its contents when power is lost; it has two main disadvantages: it is slower, and it eventually wears out. Flash memory is frequently found in PCMCIA cards.

font
In a simplistic sense, a font can be thought of as the physical description of a character set. While the character set will define what sets of bits map to what letters, numbers, and other symbols, the font will define what each letter, number, and other symbol looks like. Fonts can be either fixed width or variable width and independently, either bitmapped or vectored. The size of the large characters in a font is typically measured in points.

FORTRAN
FORTRAN stands for formula translation and is the oldest computer language in the world. Today languages like C and Java are more popular, but FORTRAN is still heavily used in military software. It is somewhat amusing to note that when FORTRAN was first released back in 1958 its advocates thought that it would mean the end of software bugs. In truth of course by making the creation of more complex software practical, computer languages have merely created new types of software bugs.

FreeBSD
A free variant of Berkeley UNIX available for Alpha and x86 based machines. It was not as popular as Linux.

freeware
Freeware is software that is available for free with no strings attached. The quality is often superb as the authors are also generally users.

FTP
The file transfer protocol is one of the most commonly used methods of copying files across the Internet. It has its origins on UNIX machines, but has been adapted to almost every type of

computer in existence and is built into many browsers. Most FTP programs have two modes of operation, ASCII, and binary. Transmitting an ASCII file via the ASCII mode of operation is more efficient and cleaner. Transmitting a binary file via the ASCII mode of operation will result in a broken binary file. Thus the FTP programs that do not support both modes of operation will typically only do the binary mode, as binary transfers are capable of transferring both kinds of data without corruption.

gateway
A gateway connects otherwise separate computer networks.

GHz & gigahertz
One gigahertz is equivalent to 1000 megahertz, or 1,000,000,000 hertz.

GNOME
The GNU network object model environment was a popular free window manager (and much more -- as its name touts, it is more of a desktop environment) that ran under X-Windows. It was a part of the GNU project.

GNU
GNU stands for GNU's not UNIX and is thus a recursive acronym (and unlike the animal name, the "G" here is pronounced). At any rate, the GNU project is an effort by the Free Software Foundation (FSF) to make all of the traditional UNIX utilities free for whoever wants them.

HP-UX
HP-UX is the version of UNIX designed by Hewlett-Packard to work with their PA-RISC and 68xx based machines.

HTML
The Hypertext Mark-up Language is the language currently most frequently used to express web pages. Every browser has the built-in ability to understand HTML. Some browsers can additionally understand Java and browse FTP areas. HTML is a proper subset of SGML.

http
The hypertext transfer protocol is the native protocol of browsers and is most typically used to transfer HTML formatted files. The secure version is called "https".

Hz & hertz
Hertz means cycles per second, and makes no assumptions about what is cycling. So, for example, if a fluorescent light flickers once per jiffy, it has a 60 Hz flicker. More typical for computers would be a program that runs once per jiffy and thus has a 60 Hz frequency, or larger units of hertz like kHz, MHz, GHz, or THz.

iCalendar
The iCalendar standard refers to the format used to store calendar type information (including events, to-do items, and journal entries) on the Internet. iCalendar data can be found on some World-Wide-Web pages or attached to e-mail messages.

icon
A small graphical display representing an object, action, or modifier of some sort.

Inform
A compiled, object-oriented language optimized for creating interactive fiction.

infrared communications
A device with an infrared port can communicate with other devices at a distance by beaming infrared light signals. Two incompatible protocols are used for infrared communications: IrDA and ASK. Many devices support both.

Instant Messenger
AOL's Instant Messenger was a means of chatting over the Internet in real-time. It allowed both open group discussions and private conversations. Instant Messenger used a different, proprietary protocol from the more standard IRC, and was not supported on as many platforms.

interactive fiction
Interactive fiction (often abbreviated "IF" or "I-F") is a form of literature unique to the computer. While the reader cannot influence the direction of a typical story, the reader plays a more active role in an interactive fiction story and completely controls its direction. Interactive fiction works come in all the sizes and genres available to standard fiction, and in fact are not always even fiction per se (interactive tutorials exist and are slowly becoming more common).

interpreted
If a program is interpreted, its actual human-readable source is read as it is run by the computer. This is generally a slower process than if the program being run has already been compiled.

Intranet
An intranet is a private network. There are many intranets scattered all over the world. Some are connected to the Internet via gateways.

IP
IP is the family of protocols that makes up the Internet.

IRC
Internet relay chat is a means of chatting over the Internet in real-time. It allows both open group discussions and private conversations.

IrDA
The Infrared Data Association (IrDA) is a voluntary organization of various manufacturers working together to ensure that the infrared communications between different computers, printers, digital cameras, remote controls, etc. are all compatible with each other regardless of brand. The term is also often used to designate an IrDA compliant infrared communications port on a device. Informally, a device able to communicate via IrDA compliant infrared is sometimes simply said to "have IrDA". There is also an earlier, incompatible, and usually slower type of infrared communications still in use called ASK.

IRI
An Internationalized Resource Identifier is just a URI with il8n.

IRIX
The variant of UNIX designed by Silicon Graphics, Inc. IRIX machines are known for their graphics capabilities and were initially optimized for multimedia applications.

ISDN
An integrated service digital network line can be simply looked at as a digital phone line. ISDN connections to the Internet can be four times faster than the fastest regular phone connection, and because it is a digital connection a modem is not needed. Any computer hooked up to ISDN will typically require other special equipment in lieu of the modem, however. Also, both phone companies and ISPs charge more for ISDN connections than regular modem connections.

ISP
An Internet service provider is a company that provides Internet support for other entities.

Java
A computer language designed to be both fairly lightweight and extremely portable. It is tightly bound to the web as it is the primary language for web applets. There has also been an OS based on Java for use on small hand-held, embedded, and network computers. It is called JavaOS. Java can be either interpreted or compiled. For web applet use it is almost always interpreted. While its interpreted form tends not to be very fast, its compiled form can often rival languages like C++ for speed. It is important to note however that speed is not Java's primary purpose -- raw speed is considered secondary to portabilty and ease of use.

JavaScript
JavaScript (in spite of its name) has nothing whatsoever to do with Java (in fact, it's arguably more like Newton Script than Java). JavaScript is an interpreted language built into a browser to

provide a relatively simple means of adding interactivity to web pages. It is only supported on a few different browsers, and tends not to work exactly the same on different versions. Thus its use on the Internet is somewhat restricted to fairly simple programs. On intranets where there are usually fewer browser versions in use, JavaScript has been used to implement much more complex and impressive programs.

jiffy
A jiffy is 1/60 of a second. Jiffies are to seconds as seconds are to minutes.

joystick
A joystick is a physical device typically used to control objects on a computer screen. It is frequently used for games and sometimes used in place of a mouse. Today, joysticks are used for gaming, robotics, medical research, virtual reality (VR), and industrial control systems.

JSON
The JSON is used for data interchange between programs, an area in which the ubiquitous XML is not too well-suited. JSON is lightweight and works extremely cleanly with languages including JavaScript, Python, Java, C++, and many others.

JSON-RPC
JSON-RPC is like XML-RPC but is significantly more lightweight since it uses JSON in lieu of XML.

kernel
The very heart of an OS is often called its kernel. It will usually (at minimum) provide some libraries that give programmers access to its various features.

kHz & kilohertz
One kilohertz is equivalent to 1000 hertz. Some older computers have clock speeds measured in kHz.

LDAP
The Lightweight Directory Access Protocol provides a means of sharing address book type of information across an intranet or even across the Internet. Note too that "address book type of information" here is pretty broad; it often includes not just human addresses, but machine addresses, printer configurations, and similar.

library
A selection of routines used by programmers to make computers do particular things.

lightweight
Something that is lightweight will not consume computer resources (such as RAM and disk space) too much and will thus run on less expensive computer systems.

Linux
One of the fastest, most robust, and powerful multitasking OS systems. Linux can be downloaded for free or be purchased for a small service charge. Linux is available for more hardware combinations than any other OS. Fast, reliable, stable, and inexpensive, Linux is popular with ISPs, software developers, and home hobbyists alike.

load
There are two popular meanings for load. The first means to fetch some data or a program from a disk and store it in memory. The second indicates the amount of work a component (especially a processor) is being made to do.

Logo
Logo is an interpreted language designed by Papert in 1966 to be a tool for helping people (especially kids) learn computer programming concepts. In addition to being used for that purpose, it is often used as a language for controlling mechanical robots and other similar devices. Logo interfaces even exist for building block / toy robot sets. Logo uses a special graphics cursor called "the turtle", and Logo is itself sometimes called "Turtle Graphics". Logo is quite portable but not particularly fast. Versions can be found on almost every computer platform in the world. Additionally, some other languages (notably some Pascal versions) provide Logo-

like interfaces for graphics-intensive programming.

lossy

If a process is lossy, it means that a little quality is lost when it is performed. If a format is lossy, it means that putting data into that format (or possibly even manipulating it in that format) will cause some slight loss. Lossy processes and formats are typically used for performance or resource utilization reasons. The opposite of lossy is lossless.

Lua

Lua is a simple interpreted language. It is extremely portable, and free versions exist for most platforms.

Mac OS

Mac OS is the OS used on Macintosh computers. There are two distinctively different versions of it; everything prior to version 10 (sometimes called Mac OS Classic) and everything version 10 or later (called Mac OS X).

Mac OS Classic

The OS created by Apple and originally used by Macs is frequently (albeit slightly incorrectly) referred to as Mac OS Classic (officially Mac OS Classic is this original OS running under the modern Mac OS X in emulation. Mac OS combines the functionality of both an OS and a window manager and is often considered to be the easiest OS to use. It is partially multitasking but will still sometimes crash when dealing with a buggy program. It is probably the second most popular OS, next only to Windows 'XP (although it is quickly losing ground to Mac OS X) and has excellent driver support and boasts a fair selection of games. Mac OS will run on PowerPC and 68xx based machines.

Mac OS X

Mac OS X (originally called Rhapsody) is the industrial strength OS produced by Apple to run on both PowerPC and x86 systems (replacing what is often referred to as Mac OS Classic. Mac OS X is at its heart a variant of UNIX and possesses its underlying power (and the ability to run many of the traditional UNIX tools, including the GNU tools).

machine language

Machine language consists of the raw numbers that can be directly understood by a particular processor. Each processor's machine language will be different from other processors' machine language. Although called "machine language", it is not usually what people think of when talking about computer languages. Machine language dressed up with mnemonics to make it a bit more human-readable is called assembly language.

Macintosh

A Macintosh (or a Mac for short) is a computer system that has Mac OS for its OS. There are a few different companies that have produced Macs, but by far the largest is Apple. The oldest Macs are based on the 68xx processor; somewhat more recent Macs on the PowerPC processor, and current Macs on the x86 processor. The Macintosh was really the first general purpose computer to employ a GUI.

MacTel

An x86 based system running some flavor of Mac OS.

mainframe

A mainframe is any computer larger than a small piece of furniture. A modern mainframe is more powerful than a modern workstation, but more expensive and more difficult to maintain.

MathML

The Math Mark-up Language is a subset of XML used to represent mathematical formulae and equations. Typically it is found embedded within XHTML documents, although as of this writing not all popular browsers support it.

megahertz

A million cycles per second, abbreviated MHz. This is often used misleadingly to indicate processor speed, because while one might expect that a higher number would indicate a faster processor, that logic only holds true within a given type of processors as different types of processors are capable of doing different amounts of work within a cycle. For a current example, either a 200 MHz PowerPC or a 270 MHz SPARC will outperform a 300 MHz Pentium.

middleware
Software designed to sit in between an OS and applications. Common examples are Java and Tcl/Tk.

MIME
The multi-purpose Internet mail extensions specification describes a means of sending non-ASCII data (such as images, sounds, foreign symbols, etc.) through e-mail. It commonly utilizes bcode.

MMX
Multimedia extensions were built into some x86 CPUs to provide better performance for certain operations, most notably graphics and sound. It is similar to AltiVec on the PowerPC CPUs. Like AltiVec, it requires special software for full performance benefits to be realized.

MOB
A movable object is a graphical object that is manipulated separately from the background. These are seen all the time in computer games. When implemented in hardware, MOBs are sometimes called sprites.

Modula-2 & Modula-3
Modula-2 is a procedural language based on Pascal by its original author in around the 1977 1979 time period. Modula-3 is an intended successor that adds support for object-oriented constructs (among other things). Modula-2 can be either compiled or interpreted, while Modula-3 tends to be just a compiled language.

MOTD
A message **of** the day. Many computers (particularly more capable ones) are configured to display a MOTD when accessed remotely.

MS-DOS
The DOS produced by Microsoft. Early versions of it bear striking similarities to the earlier CP/M, but it utilizes simpler commands. It provides only a CLI, but either OS/2, Windows 3.1, Windows '95, Windows '98, Windows ME, or GEOS may be run on top of it to provide a GUI. It only runs on x86 based machines.

MS-Windows
MS-Windows is the name collectively given to several somewhat incompatible OSes all produced by Microsoft. The latest Windows update is Windows 11, version 23H2.

MUD
A multi-user dimension (also sometimes called multi-user dungeon, but in either case abbreviated to "MUD") is sort of a combination between the online chatting abilities provided by something like IRC and a role-playing game. A MUD built with object oriented principles in mind is called a "Multi-user dimension object-oriented", or MOO. Yet another variant is called a "multi-user shell", or MUSH. Still other variants are called multi-user role-playing environments (MURPE) and multi-user environments (MUSE). There are probably more. In all cases the differences will be mostly academic to the regular user, as the same software is used to connect to all of them. Software to connect to MUDs can be found for most platforms, and there are even Java based ones that can run from within a browser.

multitasking
Some OSes have built into them the ability to do several things at once. This is called multitasking, and has been in use since the late sixties / early seventies. Since this ability is built into the software, the overall system will be slower running two things at once than it will be running just one thing. A system may have more than one processor built into it though, and such a system will be capable of running multiple things at once with less of a performance hit.

nagware
Nagware is a variant of shareware that will frequently remind its users to register.

NetBSD
A free variant of Berkeley UNIX available for Alpha, x86, 68xx, PA-RISC, SPARC, PowerPC, ARM, and many other types of machines. Its emphasis is on portability.

newbie
A newbie is a novice to the online world or computers in general.

news
Usenet news can generally be thought of as public e-mail as that is generally the way it behaves. In reality, it is implemented by different software and is often accessed by different programs. Different newsgroups adhere to different topics, and some are "moderated", meaning that humans will try to manually remove off-topic posts, especially spam. Most established newsgroups have a FAQ, and people are strongly encouraged to read the FAQ prior to posting.

Newton
Although Newton is officially the name of the lightweight OS developed by Apple to run on its MessagePad line of PDAs, it is often used to mean the MessagePads (and compatible PDAs) themselves and thus the term "Newton OS" is often used for clarity. The Newton OS is remarkably powerful; it is fully multitasking in spite of the fact that it was designed for small machines. It is optimized for hand-held use, but will readily transfer data to all manner of desktop machines. Historically it was the first PDA. Recently Apple announced that it will discontinue further development of the Newton platform, but will instead work to base future hand-held devices on either Mac OS or Mac OS X with some effort dedicated to making the new devices capable of running current Newton programs.

Newton book
Newton books provide all the functionality of ordinary books but add searching and hypertext capabilities. The format was invented for the Newton to provide a means of making volumes of data portable, and is particularly popular in the medical community as most medical references are available as Newton books and carrying around a one pound Newton is preferable to carrying around twenty pounds of books, especially when it comes to looking up something. In addition to medical books, numerous references, most of the classics, and many contemporary works of fiction are available as Newton books. Most fiction is available for free, most references cost money. Newton books are somewhat more capable than the similar Palm DOC; both are specific types of e-books.

nybble
A nybble is half a byte, or four bits. It is a case of computer whimsy; it only stands to reason that a small byte should be called a nybble. Some authors spell it with an "i" instead of the "y", but the "y" is the original form.

object-oriented
The term "object-oriented" applies to a philosophy of software creation. Often this philosophy is referred to as object-oriented design (sometimes abbreviated as OOD), and programs written with it in mind are referred to as object-oriented programs (often abbreviated OOP). Programming languages designed to help facilitate it are called object-oriented languages (sometimes abbreviated as OOL) and databases built with it in mind are called object-oriented databases (sometimes abbreviated as OODB or less fortunately OOD). The general notion is that an object-oriented approach to creating software starts with modeling the real-world problems trying to be solved in familiar real-world ways, and carries the analogy all the way down to structure of the program. This is of course a great over-simplification. Numerous object-oriented programming languages exist including: Java, C++, Modula-2, Newton Script, and ADA.

Objective-C & ObjC
Objective-C (often called "ObjC" for short) is a compiled object-oriented language. Based heavily on C, Objective-C is nearly as fast and can often be thought of as being just C with added features. Note that it was developed independently of C++; its object-oriented extensions are more in the style of Smalltalk. It is however related to Objective-C++.

Objective-C++ & ObjC++

Objective-C++ (often called "ObjC++" for short) is a curious hybrid of Objective-C and C++, allowing the syntax of both to coexist in the same source files.

office suite
An office suite is a collection of programs including at minimum a word processor, spreadsheet, drawing program, and minimal database program. Some popular office suites include Google Workspace, Microsoft 365, iWork, LibreOffice, Polaris Office and OpenOffice.

open source
Open source software goes one step beyond freeware. Not only does it provide the software for free, it provides the original source code used to create the software. Thus, curious users can poke around with it to see how it works, and advanced users can modify it to make it work better for them. By its nature, open source software is pretty well immune to all types of computer virus.

OpenBSD
A free variant of Berkeley UNIX available for Alpha, x86, 68xx, PA-RISC, SPARC, and PowerPC based machines. Its emphasis is on security.

OpenDocument & ODF
OpenDocument (or ODF for short) is the suite of open, XML-based office suite application formats defined by the OASIS consortium. It defines a platform-neutral, non-proprietary way of storing documents.

OpenGL
A low-level 3D graphics library with an emphasis on speed developed by SGI.

OS/2
OS/2 is the OS designed by IBM to run on x86 based machines. It is semi-compatible with MS-Windows. IBM's more industrial strength OS is called AIX.

Palm Pilot
The Palm Pilot (also called both just Palm and just Pilot, officially now just Palm) was the most popular PDA in use. It was one of the least capable PDAs but also one of the smallest and least expensive. While not as full-featured as many of the other PDAs (such as the Newton), it performed what features it did have quite well.

parallel
Loosely speaking, parallel implies a situation where multiple things can be done simultaneously, like having multiple check-out lines each serving people all at once. Parallel connections are by their nature more expensive than serial ones, but usually faster. Also, in a related use of the word, often multitasking computers are said to be capable of running multiple programs in parallel.

partition
Sometimes due to hardware limitations, disks have to be divided into smaller pieces. These pieces are called partitions.

Pascal
Named after the mathematician Blaise Pascal, Pascal is a language designed by Niklaus Wirth originally in 1968 (and heavily revised in 1972) mostly for purposes of education and training people how to write computer programs. It is a typically compiled language but is still usually slower than C or FORTRAN. Wirth also created a more powerful object-oriented Pascal-like language called Modula-2.

PC-DOS
The DOS produced by IBM designed to work like MS-DOS. Early versions of it bear striking similarities to the earlier CP/M, but it utilizes simpler commands. It provides only a CLI, but either Windows 3.1 or GEOS may be run on top of it to provide a GUI. It only runs on x86 based machines.

PCMCIA
The Personal Computer Memory Card International Association is a standards body that concern themselves with PC Card technology. Often the PC Cards themselves are referred

to as "PCMCIA cards". Frequently flash memory can be found in PC card form.
Perl
Perl is an interpreted language extremely popular for web applications.
PET
The Commodore PET (Personal Electronic Transactor) is an early (circa 1977-1980, around the same time as the Apple][) home computer featuring a ROM-based BASIC developed by Microsoft which it uses as a default "OS". It is based on the 65xx family of processors and is the precursor to the VIC-20.
PHP
Named with a recursive acronym (PHP: Hypertext Preprocessor), PHP provides a means of creating web pages that dynamically modify themselves on the fly.
ping
Ping is a protocol designed to check across a network to see if a particular computer is "alive" or not. Computers that recognize the ping will report back their status. Computers that are down will not report back anything at all.
pixel
The smallest distinct point on a computer display is called a pixel.
plug-in
A plug-in is a piece of software designed not to run on its own but rather work in cooperation with a separate application to increase that application's abilities.
point
There are two common meanings for this word. The first is in the geometric sense; a position in space without size. Of course as applied to computers it must take up some space in practice (even if not in theory) and it is thus sometimes synonymous with pixel. The other meaning is related most typically to fonts and regards size. The exact meaning of it in this sense will unfortunately vary somewhat from person to person, but will often mean 1/72 of an inch. Even when it does not exactly mean 1/72 of an inch, larger point sizes always indicate larger fonts.
PowerPC
The PowerPC is a RISC processor developed in a collaborative effort between IBM, Apple, and Motorola. It is currently produced by a few different companies, of course including its original developers. A few different OSes run on PowerPC based machines, including Mac OS, AIX, Solaris, Windows NT, Linux, Mac OS X, BeOS, and AmigaOS. At any given time, the fastest processor in the world is usually either a PowerPC or an Alpha, but sometimes SPARCs and PA-RISCs make the list, too.
proprietary
This simply means to be supplied by only one vendor. It is commonly misused. Currently, most processors are non-proprietary, some systems are non-proprietary, and every OS (except for arguably Linux) is proprietary.
protocol
A protocol is a means of communication used between computers. As long as both computers recognize the same protocol, they can communicate without too much difficulty over the same network or even via a simple direct modem connection regardless whether or not they are themselves of the same type. This means that WinTel boxes, Macs, Amigas, UNIX machines, etc., can all talk with one another provided they agree on a common protocol first.
queue
A queue is a waiting list of things to be processed. Many computers provide printing queues, for example. If something is being printed and the user requests that another item be printed, the second item will sit in the printer queue until the first item finishes printing at which point it will be removed from the queue and get printed itself.
RAM
Random access memory is the short-term memory of a computer. Any information stored in

RAM will be lost if power goes out, but the computer can read from RAM far more quickly than from a drive.

random access
Also called "dynamic access" this indicates that data can be selected without having to skip over earlier data first. This is the way that a CD, record, laserdisc, or DVD will behave -- it is easy to selectively play a particular track without having to fast forward through earlier tracks. The other common behavior is called sequential access.

RDF
The Resource Description Framework is built upon an XML base and provides a more modern means of accessing data from Internet resources. It can provide metadata (including annotations) for web pages making (among other things) searching more capable. It is also being used to refashion some existing formats like RSS and iCalendar; in the former case it is already in place (at least for newer RSS versions), but it is still experimental in the latter case.

real-time
Something that happens in real-time will keep up with the events around it and never give any sort of "please wait" message.

Rexx
The Restructured Extended Executor is an interpreted language designed primarily to be embedded in other applications in order to make them consistently programmable, but also to be easy to learn and understand.

RISC
Reduced instruction set computing is one of the two main types of processor design in use today, the other being CISC. The fastest processors in the world today are all RISC designs. There are several popular RISC processors, including Alphas, ARMs, PA-RISCs, PowerPCs, and SPARCs.

robot
A robot (or 'bot for short) in the computer sense is a program designed to automate some task, often just sending messages or collecting information. A spider is a type of robot designed to traverse the web performing some task (usually collecting data).

robust
The adjective robust is used to describe programs that are better designed, have fewer bugs, and are less likely to crash.

ROM
Read-only memory is similar to RAM only cannot be altered and does not lose its contents when power is removed.

RSS
RSS stands for either Rich Site Summary, Really Simple Syndication, or **RDF** Site Summary, depending upon whom you ask. The general idea is that it can provide brief summaries of articles that appear in full on a web site. It is well-formed XML, and newer versions are even more specifically well-formed RDF.

Ruby
Ruby is an interpreted, object-oriented language. Ruby was fairly heavily influenced by Perl, so people familiar with that language can typically transition to Ruby easily.

scanner
A scanner is a piece of hardware that will examine a picture and produce a computer file that represents what it sees. A digital camera is a related device. Each has its own limitations.

script
A script is a series of OS commands. The term "batch file" means much the same thing, but is a bit dated. Typically the same sort of situations in which one would say DOS instead of OS, it would also be appropriate to say batch file instead of script. Scripts can be run like programs, but tend to perform simpler tasks. When a script is run, it is always interpreted.

SCSI
Loosely speaking, a disk format sometimes used by MS-Windows, Mac OS, AmigaOS, and (almost always) UNIX. Generally SCSI is superior (but more expensive) to IDE, but it varies somewhat with system load and the individual SCSI and IDE components themselves. The quick rundown is that: SCSI-I and SCSI-II will almost always outperform IDE; EIDE will almost always outperform SCSI-I and SCSI-II; SCSI-III and UltraSCSI will almost always outperform EIDE; and heavy system loads give an advantage to SCSI. Note that although loosely speaking it is just a format difference, it is deep down a hardware difference.

sequential access
This indicates that data cannot be selected without having to skip over earlier data first. This is the way that a cassette or video tape will behave. The other common behavior is called random access.

serial
Loosely speaking, serial implies something that has to be done linearly, one at a time, like people being served in a single check-out line. Serial connections are by their nature less expensive than parallel connections (including things like SCSI) but are typically slower.

server
A server is a computer designed to provide various services for an entire network. It is typically either a workstation or a mainframe because it will usually be expected to handle far greater loads than ordinary desktop systems. The load placed on servers also necessitates that they utilize robust OSes, as a crash on a system that is currently being used by many people is far worse than a crash on a system that is only being used by one person.

SGML
The Standard Generalized Mark-up Language provides an extremely generalized level of mark-up. More common mark-up languages like HTML and XML are actually just popular subsets of SGML.

shareware
Shareware is software made for profit that allows a trial period before purchase. Typically shareware can be freely downloaded, used for a period of weeks (or sometimes even months), and either purchased or discarded after it has been learned whether or not it will satisfy the user's needs.

shell
A CLI designed to simplify complex OS commands. Some OSes (like AmigaOS, the Hurd, and UNIX) have built-in support to make the concurrent use of multiple shells easy. Common shells include the Korn Shell (ksh), the Bourne Shell (sh or bsh), the Bourne-Again Shell, (bash or bsh), the C-Shell (csh), etc.

SIMM
A physical component used to add RAM to a computer. Similar to, but incompatible with, DIMMs.

Smalltalk
Smalltalk is an efficient language for writing computer programs. Historically it is one of the first object-oriented languages, and is not only used today in its pure form but shows its influence in other languages like Objective-C.

spam
Generally spam is unwanted, unrequested e-mail or some other form of contact. It is typically sent out in bulk to huge address lists that were automatically generated by various robots endlessly searching the Internet and newsgroups for things that resemble e-mail addresses.

SPARC
The SPARC was a RISC processor developed by Sun.

sprite
The term sprite originally referred to a small MOB, usually implemented in hardware. Lately it

is also being used to refer to a single image used piecemeal within a Web site in order to avoid incurring the time penalty of downloading multiple files.

SQL
SQL (pronounced Sequel) is an interpreted language specially designed for database access. It is supported by virtually every major modern database system.

SVG
Scalable Vector Graphics data is an XML file that is used to hold graphical data that can be resized without loss of quality. SVG data can be kept in its own file, or even embedded within a web page (although not all browsers are capable of displaying such data).

Tonic
The Tool Command Language is a portable interpreted computer language designed to be easy to use. Tk is a GUI toolkit for Tcl. Tcl is a fairly popular language for both integrating existing applications and for creating Web applets (note that applets written in Tcl are often called Tcklets). Tcl/Tk is available for free for most platforms, and plug-ins are available to enable many browsers to play Tcklets.

TCP/IP
TCP/IP is a protocol for computer networks. The Internet is largely built on top of TCP/IP (it is the more reliable of the two primary Internet Protocols -- TCP stands for Transmission Control Protocol).

terminator
A terminator is a dedicated device used to mark the end of a device chain (as is most typically found with SCSI devices). If such a chain is not properly terminated, weird results can occur.

TEX
TEX (pronounced "tek") is a freely available, industrial strength typesetting program that can be run on many different platforms. These qualities make it exceptionally popular in schools, and frequently software developed at a university will have its documentation in TEX format. TEX is not limited to educational use, though; many professional books were typeset with TEX. TEX's primary drawback is that it can be quite difficult to set up initially.

THz & terahertz
One terahertz is equivalent to 1000 gigahertz.

TrackBack
TrackBacks essentially provide a means whereby different web sites can post messages to one another not just to inform each other about citations, but also to alert one another of related resources. Typically, a blog may display quotations from another blog through the use of TrackBacks.

UDP/IP
UDP/IP is a protocol for computer networks. It is the faster of the two primary Internet Protocols. UDP stands for User Datagram Protocol.

Unicode
The Unicode character set is a superset of the ASCII character set with provisions made for handling international symbols and characters from other languages. Unicode is sixteen bit, so takes up roughly twice the space as simple ASCII, but is correspondingly more flexible.

UNIX
UNIX is a family of OSes, each being made by a different company or organization but all offering a very similar look and feel. It cannot quite be considered non-proprietary, however, as the differences between different vendor's versions can be significant (it is still generally possible to switch from one vendor's UNIX to another without too much effort; today the differences between different UNIXes are similar to the differences between the different MS-Windows; historically there were two different UNIX camps, Berkeley / BSD and AT&T / System V, but the assorted vendors have worked together to minimize the differences). The free variant Linux is one of the closest things to a current, non-proprietary OS; its development is controlled by a non-profit organization and its distribution is provided by several companies. UNIX is powerful; it is

fully multitasking and can do pretty much anything that any OS can do (look to the Hurd if you need a more powerful OS). With power comes complexity, however, and UNIX tends not to be overly friendly to beginners (although those who think UNIX is difficult or cryptic apparently have not used CP/M). Window managers are available for UNIX (running under X-Windows) and once properly configured common operations will be almost as simple on a UNIX machine as on a Mac. Out of all the OSes in current use, UNIX has the greatest range of hardware support. It will run on machines built around many different processors.

upload
To upload a file is to copy it from your computer to a remote computer. The opposite is download.

UPS
An uninterrupted power supply uses heavy duty batteries to help smooth out its input power source.

URI
A Uniform Resource Identifier is basically just a unique address for almost any type of resource. It is similar to but more general than a URL; in fact, it may also be a URN.

URL
A Uniform Resource Locator is basically just an address for a file that can be given to a browser. It starts with a protocol type (such as http, ftp, or gopher) and is followed by a colon, machine name, and file name in UNIX style. Optionally an octothorpe character "#" and and arguments will follow the file name; this can be used to further define position within a page and perform a few other tricks. Similar to but less general than a URI.

URN
A Uniform Resource Name is basically just a unique address for almost any type of resource unlike a URL it will probably not resolve with a browser.

USB
A really fast type of serial port that offers many of the best features of SCSI without the price. Faster than many types of parallel port, a single USB port is capable of chaining many devices without the need of a terminator. USB is much slower (but somewhat less expensive) than FireWire.

uucode
The point of uucode is to allow 8-bit binary data to be transferred through the more common 7-bit ASCII channels (most especially e-mail). The facilities for dealing with uucoded files exist for many different machine types, and the most common programs are called "uuencode" for encoding the original binary file into a 7-bit file and "uudecode" for restoring the original binary file from the encoded one. Sometimes different uuencode and uudecode programs will work in subtly different manners causing annoying compatibility problems. Bcode was invented to provide the same service as uucode but to maintain a tighter standard.

variable width
As applied to a font, variable width means that different characters will have different widths as appropriate. For example, an "i" will take up much less space than an "m". The opposite of variable width is fixed width. The terms "proportional width" and "proportionally spaced" mean the same thing as variable width. Some common variable width fonts include Times, Helvetica, and Bookman.

vector
This term has two common meanings. The first is in the geometric sense: a vector defines a direction and magnitude. The second concerns the formatting of fonts and images. If a font is a vector font or an image is a vector image, it is defined as lines of relative size and direction rather than as collections of pixels (the method used in bitmapped fonts and images). This makes it easier to change the size of the font or image, but puts a bigger load on the device that has to display the font or image. The term "outline font" means the same thing as vector font.

VIC-20
The Commodore VIC-20 computer sold millions of units and is generally considered to have been the first affordable home computer. It features a ROM-based BASIC and uses it as a default "OS". It is based on the 65xx family of processors. VIC (in case you are wondering) can stand for either video interface **c** or video interface computer. The VIC-20 is the precursor to the C64/128.

virtual machine
A virtual machine is a machine completely defined and implemented in software rather than hardware. It is often referred to as a "runtime environment"; code compiled for such a machine is typically called bytecode.

virtual memory
This is a scheme by which disk space is made to substitute for the more expensive RAM space. Using it will often enable a comptuer to do things it could not do without it, but it will also often result in an overall slowing down of the system. The concept of swap space is very similar.

virtual reality
Virtual reality (often called VR for short) is generally speaking an attempt to provide more natural, human interfaces to software. It can be as simple as a pseudo 3D interface or as elaborate as an isolated room in which the computer can control the user's senses of vision, hearing, and even smell and touch.

virus
A virus is a program that will seek to duplicate itself in memory and on disks, but in a subtle way that will not immediately be noticed. A computer on the same network as an infected computer or that uses an infected disk (even a floppy) or that downloads and runs an infected program can itself become infected. A virus can only spread to computers of the same platform. For example, on a network consisting of a WinTel box, a Mac, and a Linux box, if one machine acquires a virus the other two will probably still be safe.

VMS
The industrial strength OS that runs on VAXen.

VoIP
VoIP means "Voice over IP" and it is quite simply a way of utilizing the Internet (or even in some cases intranets) for telephone conversations. The primary motivations for doing so are cost and convenience as VoIP is significantly less expensive than typical telephone long distance packages, plus one high speed Internet connection can serve for multiple phone lines.

VRML
A Virtual Reality Modeling Language file is used to represent VR objects. It has essentially been superceded by X3D.

W3C
The World Wide Web Consortium (usually abbreviated W3C) is a non-profit, advisory body that makes suggestions on the future direction of the World Wide Web, HTML, CSS, and browsers.

Waba
An extremely lightweight subset of Java optimized for use on PDAs.

WebDAV
WebDAV stands for Web-based Distributed Authoring and Versioning, and is designed to provide a way of editing Web-based resources in place. It serves as a more modern (and often more secure) replacement for FTP in many cases.

WebTV
A1NebTV box hooks up to an ordinary television set and displays web pages. It will not display them as well as a dedicated computer.

window manager
A window manager is a program that acts as a graphical go-between for a user and an OS. It provides a GUI for the OS. Some OSes incorporate the window manager into their own internal code, but many do not for reasons of efficiency. Some OSes partially make the division. Some

common true window managers include CDE (Common Desktop Environment), GNOME, KDE, Aqua, OpenWindows, Motif, FVWM, Sugar, and Enlightenment. Some common hybrid window managers with OS extensions include Windows ME, Windows 98, Windows 95, Windows 3.1, OS/2 and GEOS.

WinTel
An x86 based system running some flavor of MS-Windows.

workstation
Depending upon whom you ask, a workstation is either an industrial strength desktop computer or its own category above the desktops. Workstations typically have some flavor of UNIX for their OS, but there has been a recent trend to call high-end Windows NT and Windows 2000 machines workstations, too.

WYSIWYG
What you see is what you get; an adjective applied to a program that attempts to exactly represent printed output on the screen. Related to WYSIWYM but quite different.

WYSIWYM
What you see is what you mean; an adjective applied to a program that does not attempt to exactly represent printed output on the screen, but rather defines how things are used and so will adapt to different paper sizes, etc. Related to WYSIWYG but quite different.

X-Face
X-Faces are small monochrome images embedded in headers for both provides a e-mail and news messages. Better mail and news applications will display them (sometimes automatically, sometimes only per request).

X-Windows
X-Windows provides a GUI for most UNIX systems, but can also be found as an add-on library for other computers. Numerous window managers run on top of it. It is often just called "X".

X3D
Extensible 3D Graphics data is an XML file that is used to hold three-dimensional graphical data. It is the successor to VRML.

x86
The x86 series of processors includes the Pentium, Pentium Pro, Pentium II, Pentium III, Celeron, and Athlon as well as the 786, 686, 586, 486, 386, 286, 8086, 8088, etc. It is an exceptionally popular design (by far the most popular CISC series) in spite of the fact that even its fastest model is significantly slower than the assorted RISC processors. Many different OSes run on machines built around x86 processors, including MS-DOS, Windows 3.1, Windows '95, Windows '98, Windows ME, Windows NT, Windows 2000, Windows CE, Windows XP, GEOS, Linux, Solaris, OpenBSD, NetBSD, FreeBSD, Mac OS X, OS/2, BeOS, CP/M, etc. A couple different companies produce x86 processors, but the bulk of them are produced by Intel. It is expected that this processor will eventually be completely replaced by the Merced, but the Merced development schedule is somewhat behind. Also, it should be noted that the Pentium III processor has stirred some controversy by including a "fingerprint" that will enable individual computer usage of web pages etc. to be accurately tracked.

XBL
An XML Binding Language document is used to associate executable content with an XML tag. It is itself an XML file, and is used most frequently (although not exclusively) in conjunction with XUL.

XHTML
The Extensible Hypertext Mark-up Language is essentially a cleaner, stricter version of HTML. It is a proper subset of XML.

XML
The Extensible Mark-up Language is a subset of SGML and a superset of XHTML. It is used for numerous things including (among many others) RSS and RDF.

XML-RPC
XML-RPC provides a fairly lightweight means by which one computer can execute a program on a co-operating machine across a network like the Internet. It is based on XML and is used for everything from fetching stock quotes to checking weather forcasts.
XO
The energy-efficient, kid-friendly laptop produced by the OLPC project. It runs Sugar for its window manager and Linux for its OS. It sports numerous built-in features like wireless networking, a video camera & microphone, a few USB ports, and audio in/out jacks. It comes with several educational applications (which it refers to as "Activities"), most of which are written in Python.
XSL
The Extensible Stylesheet Language is like CSS for XML. It provides a means of describing how an XML resource should be displayed.
XSLT
XSL Transformations are used to transform one type of XML into another. It is a component of XSL that can be (and often is) used independently.
XUL
An XML User-Interface Language document is used to define a user interface for an application using XML to specify the individual controls as well as the overall layout.
Z-Machine
A virtual machine optimized for running interactive fiction, interactive tutorials, and other interactive things of a primarily textual nature. Z-Machines have been ported to almost every platform in use today. Z-machine bytecode is usually called Z-code. The Glulx virtual machine is of the same idea but somewhat more modern in concept.
zip
There are three common zips in the computer world that are completely different from one another. One is a type of removable removable disk slightly larger (physically) and vastly larger (capacity) than a floppy. The second is a group of programs used for running interactive fiction. The third is a group of programs used for compression.